POSITIVITY HAPPENS

CREATING HAPPINESS AND FINDING HOPE
THROUGH THE ART OF HOLIATRY

LAURI MACKEY CHHC

ISBN: 9781981089796

This book is dedicated to my mistakes.

THANK YOU'S FOR MY READERS

Go to laurislemonadestand.com/resources for your free Art of Holiatry Resource List where you receive vetted recommendations from yours truly on books, magazines, and films on your health and body image, my favorite online resources for recipes as well as my favorite recipe books. Also included are websites to follow on the latest health research, apps or websites I recommend for weight loss and exercise, and my favorite work to do of all time - books, online lessons, and apps on developing true self-care and inner growth.

Go to laurislemonadestand.com to be added to my email subscriber list and be the first to know when the book comes out on audio and you will receive this version for free!

My 30-Day Power of Positivity Challenge at the end of this book comes with song recommendations for every day that will lift and inspire you. You will find the entire list on the last page of the challenge so that you can easily look them up rather than jumping to every day to find them all. You will also receive the link to your own pdf copy of the challenge that is all dolled up!

INTRODUCTION

One quick glance into your newsfeed on social media, the news on television or talk radio, or even a quick discussion with your friend or neighbor is enough to prove how badly positivity is needed to counterbalance the negativity of our current world. When was the last time you had a full conversation without something derogatory sneaking in? When was the last time you watched the news and the entire program was reporting on positive outcomes?

Let's take this problem and bring it a little bit closer to home, shall we? Even if you wanted to be the biggest cheerleader or proponent of positivity the world has ever seen and you're ready to be a superhero shouting from the rooftops, "There is good in this world if you only look for it!" - I believe you cannot be that person until you find the power of positivity within yourself. Let's face it, we are our own worst critics. We see all too clearly any faults, from our personalities to the shape of our bodies.

I suggest there is a way to be a Positivity Powerhouse and to do it in a fun, real-life scenario way. This book will teach you, step-by-step, in an easy-to-use format and reality-driven way, to add positivity into your DNA. To make it such a part of you that you can't help but share it with others. Think a little bit of PollyAnna mixed with the powers of Wonder Woman and you're on the right track.

I know that being positive seems hard, I've been there too. My life was full of "sucking lemons" moments. These moments come in two forms; one, they are ones you've created yourself. You chose the wrong path, made the wrong choice, you look back and you're slapping the palm of your hand onto your forehead and saying, "Doh"! Or two, these moments are ones that people made for you. No matter your past, you can still find positivity in your future.

I know what it's like to make those poor choices. I've made plenty of them! From failed marriages and bad relationships with family to not graduating high school while still a teenager. These moments could have broken my spirit. They have taught me to have pity party's of epic proportions and be used over and over again as a stumbling block in my path. But I chose to take these blocks and build a bridge to a life of positivity. That same bridge is open for you to cross as well and I want to show you how.

Using my background as a Certified Holistic Health Coach, I'd like to use what I call the Art of Holiatry (hoh-lee-a-tree) to break down being positive into bite-size chunks for you. The Art of Holiatry is a triangle consisting of three points: Physical, Psychological, and Social. The physical is about consuming nourishing foods, getting sufficient rest, and engaging in movement. The psychological component encompasses integrating your mind and spirit (or intuition). When you evaluate the physical and psychological aspects of yourself and see how these components manifest in the world, you can then look at the social leg of the triangle, which focuses on relationships.

Do you need a swift kick in the pants to get you jump-started into Positivity? The 30-Day Power of Positivity Challenge at the end of this book will give it to you. Do you want 30 new song ideas for your Positivity Playlist? You got it! Do you want to add positivity into ALL areas of your life? From Psychological to Physical to the Social? You will get 10 days to uplevel each!

I am living proof that this works. I even give you some of the juicy details in the beginning part of this book through never before heard stories of my crazy life. I've met hundreds of other women who are making this work in their lives through Lauri's Lemonade Stand, A Positivity Podcast for Women. I've Beta-tested this exact challenge with women who have seen the results of this book work in their lives.

I promise that if you make a commitment to yourself and follow the outline of the 30-Day Power of Positivity Challenge that you will see the results of finding more positivity in your life. It will not only have an impact on you personally, but you will see that others around you, your inner circle, will start to change, too. You can be the catalyst for this change that starts a ripple effect through all those who come in contact with you.

Nobody wants to be that "Negative Nelly" who thinks "well, it worked for you, but it can't work for me." Nobody wants to be the procrastinator who saves being positive for a rainy day or for when things get "really bad." Nobody wants to be the one who is thinking "I don't have time or I can't finish it and do that every day!" So what? Take 60 days to finish your 30-

day challenge. Run your own race, but don't delay your right to happiness. Why would you wait to feel happy? Be the change you want to see on those media channels! Make the change right now that can make a difference starting now. Know that you are not alone in this journey and that you can start with you. You CAN be happy!

You are one book away from making a powerful change in your life. The stories in this book will provide you with hope because if I can make it, anyone can. I believe that. Come on in and learn how I kicked negativity to the curb in what seemed like impossible situations. Then dive into the 30-Day Power of Positivity Challenge and see how you can make a difference knowing that whatever your current circumstance, there is hope and happiness as soon as you reach the back cover.

CHAPTER 1

Ready to jump in? This first chapter is going to focus on the Physical aspect of the Triangle of Holiatry which is all about nourishment and movement. In nourishment we will talk about rest and food. We will then discuss the importance of physical movement.

SLEEP/REST

Our body houses our heart and spirit. I believe these vital entities to our humanity deserve not just a shack or even a modest home - they deserve plenty of space to learn and grow. They deserve a home that has been treated well with regular maintenance, a place that is clean and tidy. I don't know about you, but in talking to lots of women we feel better when our house is in working order, our laundry is put away, the rooms are tidied up, and there's food in the fridge. If you're super blessed there's even a warm meal prepared and ready to be eaten that night.

Our first priority is not going to be food. You can survive for a time without food, days in fact if you're drinking plenty of water, so your first priority is sleep. You must get enough sleep.

Not all people need the same amount of sleep, so finding your sweet spot for functionality is the key to balance. Over years of experience and practice I know that I'm a 7-hour per night kind of gal. It This number is my sweet spot. I also know, however, that if I've worked out hard for a couple of days in a row or had a couple of days that were extra stressful with work, I'm gonna have to pull in an 8-hour night.

Of course there are always outside forces that might jump in like getting sick or traveling across the country or internationally where the time zones mess you up, but through some trial and mostly just paying attention, you can find your sweet spot with your sleep.

Once you've found that sweet spot, try to stick to it as much as possible. For example, I try to be in my bedroom and getting ready for bed at 9 pm so that I can turn the lights out by 10 pm. I've been using this routine for so many years now that I don't even set an alarm. My natural biorhythms wake me up at 6 am, and I feel ready for a new day.

For those of you who might not be able to sleep through the night I'm going to recommend naps. My friend, Sadie Nardini who is an Ultimate Wellness Expert says that the one thing she does every day without fail is to take a nap. It is a sacred time and space for her to rejuvenate and rest. Again, please focus on finding your sweet spot. Give yourself permission right now to find the rest you need that is specific and unique to you.

FOOD

Trust me, I know this is a sensitive subject. Having a conversation about the food we feed our face can be as volatile as politics and religion. I'm going to tell you my story and yes, I will stand on my soapbox a bit about my viewpoint on food, but in the end, just like everything else, the choice is yours and you get to ultimately decide what is best for you. I am just going to ask that you please be open-minded. Please know that this is my story and that you have the power to create your story however you see fit. You can still love me if we disagree. I can still love you if we disagree. And we can still be friends if we disagree.

All of my adult life I have been trying to eat healthy. I had children at an early age and wanted to feed them healthy as well. However, I also wanted to impress people with my cooking skills and I knew how to cook! Some of my specialties included white chocolate cheesecake with macadamia nuts and a pastry crust, chicken-fried steak with a gravy that never had lumps, indian fry bread with butter and honey, and seriously awesome meatloaf. As you can imagine, while these tasted divine, they were not the most balanced and healthy cuisine!

When I was 35, I began getting signs from the universe, to make some major shifts in the way I fed my body. As you may know, sometimes we have wake-up calls that change everything about something we know overnight. More often, however, change comes gradually and over time. Mine started when I had shoulder surgery and my dear friend, Kara brought me a care basket. While I don't remember everything that was in the basket, I do remember the one thing that planted a seed for change: a magazine called *Eat Clean* by Tosca Reno.

My introduction to whole foods began. This wasn't a vegan or vegetarian diet, it was a whole foods diet. The diet advocated staying as close to the whole food as possible and eliminating all processed food. Eating whole foods was a great first step to having a healthy body and an added benefit was experiencing a clarity of mind.

Not long after this time, my hubby and I decided to be better at adulting (after age 40) and to finally secure life insurance policies. In order to set up life insurance you have to give a medical history, give up your height and weight, and do lab work to check for any pre-existing conditions that quite honestly might make the insurance company pay on your policy. If they find anything, they charge you more because you are more of a risk to die early. Makes sense, right?

Now to set the stage for this, you have to know that my hubby is thin. As an example, I am 5'7" and he is 6' - we both weigh 135 lbs. No, he's not too thin and is healthy as a horse (now), but what I'm about to tell you will dispel the myth that being thin equals being healthy. When we got his blood work back from the labs his cholesterol was through the roof! Not a little higher or even in the medium range...it was way too high. High enough that our doctor wanted to put him on a statin that very day. We politely declined choosing to try changing our diet and re-testing in 6 months.

You see, we were still in the first couple years of our marriage and as I mentioned earlier, I liked to impress people with my culinary skills. I wanted to impress the hubs and was feeding him foods that were too rich for what his body needed. This was the catalyst for change that began our journey to veganism or what we like to call whole food, plant-based eating.

The shift started with eliminating red meat, then eliminating all meat. It wasn't until I started making the connection between the harmful effects of dairy on the body that the real shift started happening. I read a book by Brendan Brazier called *Thrive* in which he tells of his search for the ultimate diet to help give him an advantage in his athletic performance. He was a triathlete and he had gone vegan. I remember lying in bed, reading this book and leaning over to my husband and saying, "Honey, I think I have to do this" and him responding, "I don't think I can go there with you." And I couldn't blame him!

While everything in the book made perfect sense, my biggest worry was what I was going to eat. What would my family eat? Little did I know that my world with food was about to break wide open to eating delicious, appetizing, taste-filled wonders. I consumed books by Scott Jurek and Brendan Brazier. I looked up recipes online and starting trying new vegan cookbooks. To further my knowledge, I enrolled in a class with Dr. John McDougall and became a Starchivore. This allowed me to then teach vegan cooking classes at my local health care district.

Still, I wanted more. I took a course at eCornell University and got a certificate in plant-based nutrition and ultimately went on to become a Certified Holistic Health Coach through the Institute of Integrative Nutrition in New York.

I am happy to report that Eddy (my hubby) did not have to ever take a statin drug. His cholesterol came down on its own within 6 months. Yes, he followed me on my whole foods, plant-based, vegan diet. Eddy's healing was a miraculous testament that Hippocrates got it right when he said, "Let food be thy medicine and medicine be thy food."

I could stand on my soapbox all day long about how I believe eating a whole foods, plant-based diet is the best diet for everyone on this planet. I could cite numerous scientific studies about the harms that meat and especially dairy has on our bodies and our minds. But what I'm going to ask is that you be open-minded just enough to test this approach to health and food out yourself.

What will that look like for you? Well, that depends on you. Perhaps you will dip your toe in the water and start with Meatless Mondays. Perhaps you will be truly brave and order a cookbook that I'm going to recommend to you or you'll go online to nutritionfacts.org with Dr. Michael Greger and look at the science yourself. You'll download an app, watch a DVD, or read a book. All I'm asking is for you to check it out. Do the research yourself and decide what's best for you.

Ultimately, the goal is to feed your body with the best possible nutrients available to you so that you feel amazing! On one thing we can all agree is that we could all use more fruits and vegetables in our diet. We want that body to be clean, working properly, and able to carry you through whatever your life's mission is.

To access my Resource List go to laurislemonadestand.com/resources and enter your name and email address and it will be delivered straight to your inbox. It includes recommendations for books, movies, online research, online recipes, cookbooks, weight loss, and exercise that I have personally vetted. This resource is a virtual treasure trove of information!

MOVEMENT

Just writing about movement makes me smile. As my friend, Dr. Sandra Hanna says, "Exercise is absolutely essential to your health." Dr. Sandra Hanna is a Chiropractor and Kinesiologist who practices in Oriental Medicine, Reiki, and Yoga.

I'd like to ask another favor as we talk about movement - please be open-minded. Our bodies were designed to move so we can function properly, which means exercise is a must for everyone. Exercise and movement used to be built more organically into the average life of folks (walking to work, labor jobs), but now our society's structure has changed and many people are more sedentary as dictated by their jobs. However, I suggest that exercise is more than just going to the gym after work! In order to stay motivated, exercise should be enjoyable. Is there something out there that will make you smile in conjunction with the word *exercise*? Here are some ideas:

- Surfing
- Rock-Climbing
- Mountain Biking (single or tandem)
- Road Cycling (single or tandem or spin class)
- Stand-Up Paddleboarding
- Running or Jogging
- Walking or Hiking
- Yoga/HIIT Yoga/Pilates
- Bodybuilding/Strength Training
- Swimming
- Organized Sports like basketball, football, soccer, baseball.

I have always been active, but finding the movement that also finds my smile took some learning as an adult. In my youth, I tried all sorts of sports. Basketball for 5 years, swimming for 3, track and field, cross country, softball, 3 years of soccer. Not all of those things appeal to me now. Just like everything else in my life, I've changed.

Let me tell you a little story about mountain biking as it shows my evolution of trying something new. I share this with the hope of inspiring you try something new, too!

I enjoyed riding a bike as a kid. I had a girl's purple bike with a white banana seat and goofy handlebars with pink and purple fringe adorning the handles themselves. I recall riding that bike in a parade with colorful streamers interlaced between the spokes. In my teens, I remember borrowing my dad's green or blue ten speeds. They had cages on the pedals to hold your feet in (ridiculously dangerous looking back) and shifters that were either on the end of the handlebars or on the top tube of the bike. As an adult the only bikes I rode were in a spin class at the gym, so when my husband and I decided to buy bikes to commute to work because gas prices were skyrocketing, I knew I was in for a learning curve.

To begin our new adventure, we bought a couple of mountain bikes at a local sports store. They cost less than $200 each and because I didn't plan to go off road (ever!), we bought the mountain bikes solely for comfort and durability. They worked well and my mountain bike journey began. We started commuting to work on the roads, but pretty soon my husband was finding little dirt sections he could ride as part of our commute. I remember one downhill that seemed so frightening, I would grab handfuls of brake all the way down.

Soon after, a close friend of ours decided to show my

husband Eddy what mountain biking was all about and invited him for a "friends" ride on some local trails. Eddy was excited; I declined. I was afraid of crashing, and while I love the outdoors, I wasn't looking to become part of the landscape.

Eddy enjoyed his mountain biking experience, but when he broke his ribs on a downhill while out with his buddies, I was even more convinced that mountain biking wasn't for me. After Eddy healed, he somehow convinced me to go out on some local fire roads. For those of you who don't know, a fire road is a wide dirt road where vehicles can go while single track trails are just that...meant for a single bike or person. I actually enjoyed it! (Grudgingly, I'll admit - but it was fun!)

Pretty soon I was testing new terrain on single track trails and finding my groove on a mountain bike. I've always been a bit of a tomboy and this new form of movement felt right - like being true to my inner self kind of right. Not that I didn't have some bad days or bad moments as I began blazing down trails. I've crashed and even cracked some ribs in the process. One time, my hubby took me up a local single track trail called Space Mountain. I hated it. I hated every little part of it and I wasn't quiet about how I felt. I was upset with Eddy, cried a lot (I'm a crier, but I'll talk about that in the next chapter) and was all around pissed that he would have the audacity to take me on such a trail as this! While Space Mountain still challenges me, I can do it now without stopping or complaining. Hip, hip, hurray!

Mountain Biking has now brought me all kinds of joy. My youngest daughter joined a local high school mountain bike team for a year, and I practiced with her group. While she didn't stick with it, I am in my 5th year of head-coaching that team. I've raced in many local races and have stood on podiums with medals and trophies. I ride my mountain bike 3 days/week. I go to The Sea Otter Classic in Monterey, CA (the largest bike event in the US) every year and ride the 20-mile mountain bike Gran Fondo just because. Because I took a chance, tried something new, and persisted, I have found my joy around mountain biking.

Why do I share this with you? Because finding a passion can sometimes mean kicking resistance to the curb. I have found joy, fun, and even new friends on my mountain biking journey, and while engaging in movement and exercise doesn't have to be mountain biking for you, I encourage you to choose something! Anything! Find your passion around movement and don't let fear or a few bumps in the road stand in your way.

These days I'm not just mountain biking. I smile because every Wednesday afternoon I am on my road bike with my friend Timari as we do laps and visit a lot. If the weather is too poor, we will take yoga class (not as much talking, but I love how I feel after). I have a small home gym for strength training a couple times a week. If a camera were present, you would also see me bee-bopping around as one of my favorite songs comes on from my Gym playlist. I take the time to dance and sing out loud right in the middle of my workout because it makes me happy.

I've recently taken up hiking again because I remember how much I enjoyed climbing around on the rock piles over the levee by the Feather River as a kid. I have rediscovered the joy of nature, trail walking, and being away from pavement for a time--and this environment of exercise and movement makes me smile. I'm not doing much racing or competitive running any more because I am evolving again. I still run/jog a couple of times a week using the Active apps you can find in the resource list earlier in this chapter.

What about you? What will make you smile when you move? Find it and make it happen. Your body will reward you with great benefits.

Now that you've learned a variety of ways to sleep, nourish your body, and get movin', time to jump on over to the second point on the triangle in The Art of Holiatry which is the Psychological self. This part of the triangle includes the mind and spirit, or your secular knowledge and intuition.

CHAPTER 2

Understanding the concept of Holiatry (Hoh-lee-a-tree) is important for the next chapters. As humans, we are the sum of our parts, and while breaking down our total well-being into the triangle as suggested in the Art of Holiatry, we must remember that each aspect of the triangle works in tandem to create our unique selves as a whole.

The Art of Holiatry is broken down into three parts; Physical, Psychological, and Social. This book breaks down each individual part much like the instruments in an orchestra. Each instrument is essential and needs to be working properly and played well, but the symphony as a whole is a thing to behold.

In Holiatry, we will constantly be taking inventory and doing maintenance on all the individual parts, but we are looking for the symphony as a whole. We are human so we will never achieve perfection, however, I believe that by tuning each individual part we will be in the best shape possible to accomplish our goals, be our most authentic selves, and bring our best game to this thing we call life.

This second chapter focuses on the Psychological Triangle of Holiatry, the mind and spirit. In speaking about the mind I am talking about knowledge: education and the school of life. The spirit is our intuition, our sense of self, and self-love, which makes you unique.

MIND

I think we all agree that knowledge is power. When someone brings up the word knowledge, my brain automatically jumps to educational knowledge such as going to high school, college, a university. Sitting in a classroom and being taught by a teacher or professor. When you encounter the word knowledge, what are your first thoughts?

While my personal story is about a challenge in this realm of education, I want to clarify I understand knowledge is so much more than this. We learn through our experiences and circumstances in life. We learn through our parents, our mentors, our friends. We even learn through complete strangers. Where else do we find learning? Through the books we read, the music we listen to, the television or movies or documentaries we watch. We choose what to keep and apply to our own lives and what to toss out the window as something that is not a part of us.

When I was in high school I got attached to boys. It was more like an addiction and while it broke my mother's heart, I decided that I wanted my own family, my own house to run, my own children so that I could do it "right." Bless my mom's tender heart. She did what she could to warn me, teach me, and love me...but I was addicted to boys. So much so that I ended up getting pregnant (on purpose) just so I could have what *I wanted*. I defied my mother's and ecclesiastical leaders advice, got pregnant the summer after my sophomore year and was married by the time I started my junior year. While this is a whirlwind story, my focus is not on the story itself, but the fact that I didn't finish high school as my secular learning.

I ended up getting my GED the end of that year, and while I have not found any regrets in missing proms or establishing myself as a basketball star (I played for 5 years and while I don't know that I would have been a star - who knows?), I always missed the fact that I didn't have a diploma and didn't have a graduation ceremony with my fellow classmates.

My addiction around boys would lead me through several failed marriages until I finally had my "come to Jesus" moment and turned my faith, hope, and addiction over to God for healing. Not only did He heal me, but he brought me my perfect match of a husband, Eddy, who was the first one that I didn't choose myself, but that God hand-delivered. My choices to date had only left me with one heartache after another. Anyone who has ever suffered through addiction knows exactly what I'm talking about. I've been with Eddy for over ten years as of the writing of this book and I couldn't be happier! He has left me room to not just love him like crazy (I'm talking cheesy-crazy love here), but to explore who I am and who I want to be when I grow up.

During this journey of self-discovery I realized that there might be a possibility of tying up some of those loose ends or unfinished business from my past. Just to be clear, these moments were things I had created. I chose to get pregnant at 16 years old and have my first child at 17. I chose to take my

GED at this time. I chose these paths that left me with unfinished business that I felt needed mending later in my life. I had no one to blame but myself, but was there a way to perhaps still accomplish some of the things I had missed? Could I get my high school diploma after age 40?

Indeed, yes! The process of earning my diploma took a long time of committing, re-committing, and re-committing again. It took ridiculous hours of homework, tests, tutoring (I hadn't done algebra or geometry for over 20 years!), and pure grit. May I also add that it's way harder as an adult to graduate high school than as a teenager? If you have a teenager at home who is struggling with their classes, tell them to stick with it. Or if you haven't done it and it's a desire of yours, please do what you need to and get it done.

Not only did I graduate from Oxnard Adult School in June 2012, but I was able to speak at my graduation. All three of my daughters attended along with other family and friends. I got to wear a cap and gown! I had senior pictures taken and my dear hubby even bought me a class ring. And because the adult school was in a predominantly hispanic community (imagine me, this older white lady with graying hair attending with a bunch of hispanic teenagers and young adults - I stuck out like a sore thumb, but they were so supportive of me!), we had a mariachi band! They were dressed to the nines and I danced with all the other grads!

It's important to note that not only was this a dream come true and the ending of a goal, but I want to share with you the feeling I had at that exact moment. I felt like Wonder Woman! I felt like I could do anything and I mean anything I set my mind to. Going back to high school was no joke. If I could do this, I could get a degree, start a business, whatever I wanted to pursue, I knew without a shadow of a doubt that I could do it. I will never forget that feeling.

Since then, I have gone on to receive a Certificate in Plant-Based Nutrition from Cornell University. I've taken the Starchivore program from Dr. John McDougall and have become a Certified Holistic Health Coach through the Institute of Integrative Nutrition in New York. I have taken a Personal Finance course through our churches Self-Reliance program and am facilitating a Starting and Growing My Business course through that same Self-Reliance Program.

Two years ago, I started a Positivity Podcast for Women that is now on iTunes, Spotify, Podbean, and Soundcloud, called Lauri's Lemonade Stand and this year I'm writing my first book (thank you for supporting my journey and buying it!). Lauri's Lemonade Stand is becoming a legit business where I am reaching 1000's of women every week in encouraging them into the next chapter of their lives - whatever that may be.

All these wonderful experiences have manifested because I decided that I wanted to get my high school diploma a few years ago. What are you wanting to finish? If you are like me, I'm oh-so- good at starting all sorts of things. New ventures and ideas pop into my head daily, but for me, the challenge is finishing. I now know that on the other side of that finish line is a whole brand new list of possibilities. It is my experience that for every one thing I finish, there is at least one more waiting to help me grow in my knowledge. This can be your experience, too! Take some think time and decide what your next addition of knowledge can be for you. I believe in you!

SPIRIT

I have discovered that I function at my best when I tune in to my intuition, and I allow that inner sense to guide me in choices rather than simply following my heart. As some of you may know, following our hearts can sometimes lead us into bad relationships or situations. I'm talking about following our intuition and learning to trust ourselves. As a best practice, I believe it is important to follow our intuition and *lead* our hearts.

Our intuition can lead us to our better selves. It is wrapped around self-love, creativity, creative energy, and recess. It is wrapped around light bulb moments that you get while driving, meditation, or like me, in the shower. It can take the form of meditation, quiet time to ponder, or praying to our higher power. It can take the form of blasting rock music in your car at deafening decibels. It manifests itself through serendipitous moments or synchronicity (happy coincidences).

I'd like to share a few stories with you that will show you how I've been best able to follow my intuition by tuning out any outside noise. What is outside noise? Anything that distracts you from your true self. Media is a behemoth in this arena. Magazines portraying impossible body styles. Commercials always touting some other drug you need to be better. You know what I'm talking about. This can also be a moment as a child or teenager that left you thinking that you were a certain way, when in fact you weren't. It could be a co-worker or boss that made some derogatory comment that you've now turned into a belief system and made their statement true. Let's destroy that outside noise and find our true selves. I promise that if you start trusting your intuition that you will be able to unravel more and more of you. You will get to know yourself better and better and trust your own judgments as opposed to that outside noise.

Crying

"God grant me the serenity to accept the things I cannot change; courage to change the things I can; and wisdom to know the difference." This is the serenity prayer and the perfect quote to tell you the story of accepting something that didn't need to be changed in myself.

I am a crier. I cry when I'm freaked out, when I'm angry, when I'm sad, and occasionally even when I'm happy. It wasn't until I was fairly newly married to Eddy that I had one of my "episodes" and with hot tears streaming down my face, blurting out, "I'm going to get a handle on this! I am going to learn to control my tears" that I received the greatest gift.

My husband gently and quietly said to me, "Honey, I've known you for a long time now and I don't think this part of you is going to change." What? Do you mean to tell me that it's ok for me to be a crier? For real? All of a sudden my entire perspective changed and a weight was lifted that I had been carrying for years. IT WAS OK FOR ME TO CRY! Since that moment, I have been a catalyst in helping others embrace their emotions and their true selves.

My trying to control my crying wasn't hurting anyone but myself. I saw crying as a flaw that needed to be mended, when in actuality this is a fundamental aspect of my personality. I make zero excuses for crying now. I am a crier and I'm totally ok with that. Is there something you have been beating yourself up over that you could start embracing about yourself today? I'm gonna bet there is and that you know exactly what that something is.

Creativity

I used to say "I'm not creative." I'm talking for years I would say that. Then I read and followed the book, *The Artist's Way*, by Julia Cameron and guess what I found? I'm crazy awesome creative! What I really meant all of those years was "I'm not crafty." For example, my mother is a master seamstress, so I felt that I needed to be able to sew at least proficiently. I even went as far as signing up for a sewing class in my early 30's to sew myself a skirt. I hated it. I hated the sewing, I hated the skirt and it just confirmed the fact that "I'm not creative." No, I just didn't like sewing.

Another example of self-described lack of creativity is that I don't like to scrapbook or do crafts. I've done lots of crafts over the years and while I have a good eye for putting things together, I do not enjoy the process or outcome. Again, I confirmed to myself that "I'm not creative." It wasn't until I took Julia Cameron's course based in her book that I realized that I manifested creativity in a *bajillion* ways that I hadn't given myself credit for.

I have a beautifully decorated home in a style that didn't come out of any magazine. **I c**reated our home out of things that I loved and have collected over years. It is warm, comfy, cozy, and very inviting. That's creative. I love to write poetry. That's creative. I love to write and to speak in public. That's creative. My husband and I own a large format printing company that I give my two cents on designs regularly (much to our graphic designer's chagrin). That's creative. I just finished designing 10 lemonade t-shirts that are now on Amazon for sale. That's super creative and fun!

So, I'm not crafty. So what? I am seriously creative and guess what? SO ARE YOU! There isn't a person on this earth who doesn't have a right to creativity in some form and that includes you. How can you tap into that creativity? As Julia Cameron wrote, "Serious creativity comes from serious play." I had to learn how to take recess all over again and guess what? At first I stunk at it.

Recess

My first attempt at recess fell flat. I basically was challenged to spend an hour and a half, a total of 90 minutes by myself doing something fun. Have you ever tried planning something fun for yourself? Something where you aren't responsible for the needs of others? Well, let me tell you that my first date seriously stunk. When I think about "me time" I immediately picture someone sitting on the beach, reading a book or basking in the sun, listening to the waves. They have a sense of peace and calm, even serenity. I decided that I wanted that so I planned my first date at the beach. I was going to climb this large sand hill that I had never climbed, sit on the sand and just be.

The problem is that I don't like the beach. I live 15 minutes away from the beach in sunny Southern California and I don't like the beach. Listening to the waves is nice and even soothing, but I detest the sand. I hate how it gets in every little crevice of my clothing and in between my toes. I hate that it will end up in my car and it will need to be vacuumed. I hate when it's windy and the sand ends up in my hair and

21

blowing across any part of my body. Ya, probably not much of a beach person so why did I decide that the beach would be a good idea?

Your self-date should rejuvenate you! You should feel a sense of peace and calm or a sense of exciting fun. It should reflect who you are and it should be playful in its nature. Well, I climbed that sand hill and sat on that beach for over an hour. I watched the road below where there was a race that day and hundreds of runners walked, jogged, and ran by. And then I went home. It was boring!

The good news is that I got better at this whole self-date thing and I'm going to show you how to create your first perfect self-date by using your 5 senses as clues. I've had lots of self-dates and this is just one idea so let your imagination run wild in your creation. This is just a good springboard for new ideas later.

Creating the Perfect Self-Date

Get out a piece of paper and a pen. Write out your five senses and leave space for 3-5 answers under each heading.

Sight, Sound, Touch, Taste, Smell

Here's mine and I'll tell you about my successful self-date I created around it.

Sight

1. Horses
2. Marvel Movies
3. Any book by Josi S Kilpack or Nancy Campbell Allen
4. Comfy Fire in the Fireplace

Sound

1. The sound of the dishwasher running.
2. Running Water
3. My Awesome Playlists
4. The large printers running at work.

Touch

1. Towels right out of the dryer.
2. Soft Pillows/Throws
3. Hot Shower
4. My Love Monster (A stuffed animal on my nightstand)

Taste

1. French Fries
2. Saffron Rice/Yellow Dahl
3. Favorite Vegan Dark Chocolate Bar
4. Buttered Toast

Smell

1. Citrus Blossoms (Lemon or Orange
2. Popcorn Popping
3. Jasmine Blooms
4. Toast

Using my list, I then chose one item out of each and created a date around it. I bought a diffuser on Amazon and diffused wild orange from DoTerra. I ran to my favorite vegan fast food restaurant, Veggie Grill, and bought two kinds of french fries off the menu (yukon and sweet potato). I turned on the dishwasher which had zero dishes in it, but the sound was lovely. I had my comfy fireplace going and snuggled into my recliner with a book from Josi S Kilpack and a snuggly blanket.

While this might not do it for you, I'm betting that with your answers you can create the perfect self-date that will leave you feeling some self-love. Plan and schedule it now!

(I first heard about this concept from Rebekah Borucki, the author of *You Have 4 Minutes to Change Your Life*, who heard of it from Erin Stutland with *The Shrink Session Workout*. Both of these beautiful women have been on my podcast and have lots to offer so please check them out!)

SELF-LOVE

You have long heard the story of "putting on your own oxygen mask before helping those around you to put on theirs". You cannot give what you don't have to give. It's as simple and not easy as that. Simple in concept, harder to execute.

What does deep self-love look like to me? Being comfortable in my own skin. Knowing my own value and standing up for what I believe in. Doing more of what makes me happy and less of what doesn't. Embracing my inner freakazoid that wants to come out and be wild and play. Taking time for rest and contemplation. Less clutter and surrounding myself with things that are meaningful to me. (Even if no one understands why I keep a "Love Monster" stuffed animal on my nightstand that watches over me while I sleep). Surrounding myself with people who love and uplift me and distancing myself from those who don't. It's about being scared and doing something anyway or letting myself cry without judgment. What does deep self-love look like to you?

Self-love was not an easy thing for me to accomplish. To be honest, I'm still working on it. Let me share a story that I'm hoping you can relate to so that we, as women, can continue to show up as our best selves in the category of self-love (without any guilt whatsoever).

In one of my speeches (and for those of you who have heard me speak in conferences - my apologies, you get to hear it again), I make the entire audience my new best friend. I then tell them that I think I'm fat. I hate how I fit in my jeans. I wish I had better control over my eating. That this muffin top is hideous. I then ask them to talk to me as if we were the best of friends. What would you tell me?

Inevitably, one of the first two responses is always, "You're beautiful!" Every single time I've given that speech, those two words are one of the first two responses. Why is that? Because we love and care about our friends and we KNOW that they are beautiful, that's why. Inside, outside, all of them is beautiful.

We are our own worst critics. We all know this to be true. So why do we have such a hard time giving ourselves the same kind of slack? Why, when we are in those moments can we not look at ourselves in the mirror and say, "You're beautiful." Because we've been trained towards negative self-talk. We are constantly bombarded by how we don't measure up. From magazine ads that have photoshopped women to every other commercial on TV touting a new drug to make us better in some way. From the endless lines of make-up that showcase "anti-aging" products to the salons that cover our silver hair.

I like Cindy Joseph with BOOM! Products philosophy on aging. (You can check her out on the podcast as well since she is over 60 and an incredible model!) I told her during that interview that I was embracing my gray and that my hairdresser was mortified. Ya know what she said? "What? You're embracing your gray? Are you trying to give it a hug or something? I say we change the script. Why don't we celebrate our silver?" Well, I can't agree more! I don't want to give my gray a hug. And gray sounds so dull and bland and BORING. Today, more than ever, I am celebrating my silver! Let's not use "anti-aging" products. Let's wholeheartedly love ourselves at any age. You've earned every wrinkle and it is time to celebrate that with a flourish and grandeur.

I'm not saying changing our mindset easy. It's taken me years to change the script in my head and love the body I'm in. To find that mirror and say, "You're beautiful." Oh, I still want to be fit and not have a muffin top over my jeans, but I can now love myself no matter the current state of my body. I have always loved my freckles so I celebrate that. I love how tall I am and I celebrate that. I truly love and celebrate my silver and good thing, cause I'm getting more every year! I love my nose and my eyes. I love my feet and that I'm strong when climbing a particularly challenging hill on my mountain bike.

I'm betting you're a pretty amazing person. If I were to sit down with you right now and have a short discussion I bet that I could find some pretty incredible things about you. Give yourself some credit! Take a minute to tell yourself the things you like about yourself. Do this about your physical body and then about your personality and character traits. If you're feeling particularly brave, I double-dog-dare you to look in the mirror and say them to your face. You will probably feel silly at first, but it is an amazing experience.

TIME AND ENERGY VAMPIRES

Some have found their life callings in serving their communities and to them I give a standing ovation. I applaud your tireless efforts on our behalf and support you as much as I'm able. On the other hand, I am a deeply devoted wife, daughter, mother, friend, business owner, church member, and religiously take time for myself without guilt or hesitation, and get this - I learned how to use the word "NO" with ease.

Having said that, if you feel like it's your calling to be super-involved, by all means, bust it out and get it done. Maybe you're retired, independently wealthy, or you're like my dear neighbor - she is retired and spends a lot of her time volunteering at the local cat shelter and so it fits into her lifestyle. If you feel like you might break like a dry twig that just had a 100 lb weight put on it if someone asks you to do one more thing outside of your already packed itinerary and life, SAY NO. It's ok to say no.

It could be someone asking you to bring food to an event, setting up for an event, or volunteering to be the Girl Scout Cookie Mom for the fourth year in a row. If you don't have the bandwidth to make it happen, politely decline. It's ok. A no guilt "I appreciate you asking, but I'll have to pass this time" is perfectly acceptable. Feel free to use my mantra anytime, "Say no, then let it go".

How are you feeling so far? You've tackled the first point of the triangle in Chapter 1 which focused on your physical self. Then in Chapter 2 we jumped into our mind and spirit and learned more about ourselves than we maybe wanted to know, but we're feeling good about our future. Now onto the last Chapter where we take what we've learned and bring it into our social lives - our relationships. This includes ALL of our relationships from strangers to our lovers.

CHAPTER 3

When we learn how to support ourselves from the first two triangles of the Art of Holiatry which are Physical and Psychological, it's time to show up better to the third and last triangle, Social. This part of the triangle is all about relationships. We were built to work within families, neighborhoods, communities, and even nations. I would go so far as to say as a world family.

In this final chapter and before you head into the 30-Day Power of Positivity Challenge, we are going to talk about all sorts of relationships. I will discuss these various relationships in the following categories: strangers, romantic relationships, children, extended family, friendships, church, work, and neighbors/community.

STRANGERS

Strangers are one of my favorite categories in the social or relationship triangle. Interacting with folks we do not know can be lots of fun. Here is a list of 10 things you can do that will brighten your day and a stranger's day:

1. Say "Hi" to the person next to you in the elevator.
2. Tell someone he or she dropped a dollar (even though they didn't), then give it to them.
3. Leave a note on someone's car telling them how awesome they parked.
4. Leave a kind server the biggest tip you can afford.
5. Smile at five strangers.
6. Take flowers or treats to the nurse's station at your nearest hospital.
7. Give away stuff for free on Craigslist or Facebook Marketplace.
8. Pay it Backward: Buy the drink for the person behind you in line.
9. Let someone go in front of you in line at the store or theater.
10. Place positive body image notes in jean pockets and coats at a department store.

ROMANTIC RELATIONSHIPS

There's a song by Natasha Bedingfield called "I Love You" that pretty much sums up how I feel about my romantic relationship which is to keep it simple and that saying "I love you" is always better than over-reacting, over-analyzing, or being overbearing. You see, in the song, Natasha is looking for the perfect, "right" words to say to show her love. She's wasted tons of paper trying to come up with something. She's done research into dead poets and has tried finding the perfect combination of notes on her drum machine. She is looking for inspiration and magic, but in the end she finds that nothing says it better than the powerful simplicity of "*I LOVE YOU.*"

I have found that marriage or romantic relationships will never have true equality or fairness. Trying to split everything 50/50 or comparing what I accomplish on a day to day basis with my significant other leaves me feeling like I've always drawn the short straw. Relationships are about is giving 100% of my best, 100% of the time. Not that I'm always at a 100% level, mind you, I'm just not playing a comparison game with my husband. I have come to understand that while I can't give 100% of the time, and sometimes l hold more than my share or vice versa, it's still a good game of give and take.

I love this quote by President Gordon B Hinckley: "I am satisfied that happiness in marriage is not so much a matter of romance as it is an anxious concern for the comfort and well-being of one's companion. Any man who will make his wife's comfort his first concern will stay in love with her throughout their lives and through the eternity yet to come" (Anchorage, Alaska, regional conference, 18 June 1995).

Admittedly, I stunk in the marriage department for my first three marriages. I didn't know how to date, I knew how to get my man to the chapel - and fast! I don't recommend this route. If the people that care about you the most are seeing lots of red flags - listen to them. Maya Angelou said it best, "When someone shows you who they are, believe them the first time."

My first marriage was a teenage, high school romance. After years of experience (and therapy!) and self-reflection it wasn't hard to determine the source and why I let that rule my relationship world for a couple of decades.

31

Turns out my biological father isn't marriage material, but got married not long after high school to my mother and had four kids. I am the oldest. I'm sure he was doing his best, but when selfish desires take over and you find more interest in being outside the home instead of in, then problems will inevitably follow. While this type of absence can come in many forms, my dad spent time hunting, with his dogs, and ultimately with an 18-year-old young woman with whom he had an affair, that finally ended the marriage. I was 11 years old and to this day, my dad has never remarried.

The years that followed wreaked havoc on my psyche as my heart battled between devotion to my biological dad, who saw us maybe twice a year for an hour visit that consisted of driving to Thrifty's for a double-scoop of mint chocolate chip ice cream in a sugar cone, and trying to let my loving step-dad into my life. It shouldn't have been a battle, but for me it was quite real. In the end, I looked outside of my own family and sought to fill that void with boys.

And here's how it went down: My first marriage was a shotgun wedding because I got pregnant the summer between my sophomore and junior year of high school with my first daughter being born a couple of months after I turned 17. That incredibly rocky relationship lasted 8 years and ended with two beautiful daughters only a couple of years apart, but I hadn't healed in the least - I still had a desperate need to have a man in my life.

My second marriage was to a military man and for awhile it was really good. He had more discipline in his life and it helped me to find structure, a husband with a steady paycheck, and the amazing blessing of being a stay-at-home mom for many years. The problem was that we both had problems. You see, in the US Navy there is a cycle. You learn of the next deployment and you start to prepare. All of your time is spent in preparation and in anticipation of the departure. Then it's six months of being a single mom and very independent. Then it's almost time for the homecoming and once he arrives, it's the honeymoon period which is always fun! Then things would start to get rocky for those of us without firm marriage foundations to stand on, but pretty soon you're getting ready for the next deployment and the cycle starts again.

The problems came when we moved to Hawaii for three years and my husband was on shore duty. There's no cycle and you're spending lots of time together and learning about each other. To put it quite bluntly, this is where a couple can sink or swim. We started to sink. We realized how incompatible we were and by the time we were on to our next duty station back in San Diego, our foundations had been rocked to the core. Things got really bad and as the relationship deteriorated, so did my self-esteem. I felt ugly, unloved, unwanted, and devastated that I had yet another failing marriage. That relationship lasted 9 years and we had one beautiful daughter together during that time. I will forever be blessed to have my amazing daughters.

Enter marriage number three. I was off the rails insane with this rebound relationship! It was with a ridiculously young man who was barely of legal age, but that paid attention to me and loved me and for a woman who felt like she was in the desert of her life, it was like a well of crystal clear spring water to me. I thrived! And I was blinded. I was selfish to the hilt and didn't think about how this was affecting my daughters, the young man, my extended family, anybody or anything. Quite honestly, in the moment I didn't care. It felt so good to feel loved that I pushed everything and everyone else to the side.

Of course, this whirlwind relationship failed miserably as it had no foundational base to rely on. It was a rebound relationship pure and simple and was doomed to failure. It lasted less than a year. I had ignored the advice of my friends, family, even my clergy to the point of excommunication from my church to keep a stranglehold on this relationship. I was desperate, addicted, and not yet healed.

This is when I gave up. And I mean gave up in the best possible way. It's still hard to explain the concept of letting go to gain control. I think the best way to do that is by reviewing the 12 steps of Alcoholics Anonymous. Put simply, I replaced the addiction of alcohol with my addiction to bad relationships. Here is how the 12 Steps read for me and my addiction of choice:

1. We admitted we were powerless over our addiction– that our lives had become unmanageable.
2. Came to believe that a Power greater than ourselves could restore us to sanity.
3. Made a decision to turn our will and our lives over to the care of God as we understood Him.
4. Made a searching and fearless moral inventory of ourselves.
5. Admitted to God, to ourselves and to another human being the exact nature of our wrongs.
6. Were entirely ready to have God remove all these defects of character.
7. Humbly asked Him to remove our shortcomings.
8. Made a list of persons we had harmed, and became willing to make amends to them all.

9. Made direct amends to such people wherever possible, except when to do so would injure them or others.
10. Continued to take personal inventory and when we were wrong promptly admitted it.
11. Sought through prayer and meditation to improve our conscious contact with God as we understood Him, praying only for knowledge of His will for us and the power to carry that out.
12. Having had a spiritual awakening as the result of these steps, we tried to carry this message to others and to practice these principles in all our affairs.

Thus, this book. Step 12 is why I am writing this book. I was miserable, but I learned some things along the way that I thought might just be able to spread hope in the lives of other women.

After my rebound relationship I knew that I was powerless over my addiction. I knew that my life had become unmanageable and that the only one I had to blame was myself. I remember the evening so clearly. My daughters were visiting my second husband and I was home alone. I remember "giving up" and kneeling at the side of my bed and praying. I don't even remember praying for forgiveness at that point, I just wanted help. I was truly powerless over my addiction. My life had become unmanageable and I had no idea what to do next. I asked God for help. "Please help me to be ok on my own and without a man. Please help me to be a good mom to my kids." I remember promising that I would never ask for another man in my life as long as he helped me be ok with me. (I was such a martyr back then.)

Everything that I am and have today I can trace back to this moment. Yep, I had been married too many times and had no one to blame but myself. Yep, I had put myself and others through hell with me. By the way, if you think your decisions only affect you, you're wrong. That's just not how it works. Of course they affect those around you, especially those close to you. If you are in this vein of thinking, consider it a red flag and pay attention.

I learned (the very hard way) that my decisions affect others. With my experience of hurting others, I long to help others NOT make the same mistakes. Not listening to my family and friends brought dreadful and miserable consequences for me. They were brave enough to be honest with me about the red flags they noticed, yet I was too prideful to see their love for me. Do you have friends or family in your life offering you words of wisdom? Words that may be difficult to hear, yet you know are truth in your spirit and intuition? Sister, I urge you to listen!

It wasn't many months later that my Heavenly Father brought my current husband into my life. I wasn't looking for a relationship, didn't want it, was afraid of it, but for once, I wasn't choosing my husband. I firmly believe that God did, and ya know what? He was way better at it than I ever was!

As of the writing of this book, I've been happily married for 11 years and counting. This relationship has brought me incredible joy and a safe place to learn about who I am in this world. Eddy is my best friend and soulmate. All because I "gave up" and let God (or your higher power) assist. What is your love story?

If you are struggling in your marriage or intimate relationship, please consider looking inside yourself. Not all marriages are bliss or doomed to failure, but you are responsible for you. Please make sure that what you are doing is right and true before deciding to pursue the relationship or walk away because you're hurting each other so badly. I'm not asking you to stay in an abusive relationship. No way. But I LOVE counseling and couples therapy. It helps you to get out of your own way. Not into therapy just yet?

Here's my recommendation: Watch the movie *FireProof* and do the 40-Day Challenge called the Love Dare. I will tell you that it is based in the Christian faith so they will quote scripture, but this is a breakthrough of how you learn to "Lead your heart, instead of follow your heart." This was an entirely new concept for me, but looking back over my marriages, it was easy to see how I had "followed my heart." I learned my heart couldn't be trusted! I learned to lead my heart. Don't get me wrong, I'm happily and thoroughly in love. We are talking cheesy like crazy kinda love, but like Natasha Bedingfield, I can't find a better phrase than just telling him every day, "I Love You, period."

CHILDREN

I've been a mother my entire adult life and as of the writing of this book, all of my children are now adults, and guess what? I'm still thinking about being a better mom and how I can show up better for them in their lives. It's funny how we think we will have more time when our children are grown, but that time is quickly filled with other aspirations and dreams. That is why my best bit of advice is to BE PRESENT.

I'm really busy with writing a book, podcasting, speaking engagements, and being in a kick-ass relationship with my hubby. I like extracurricular activities like mountain biking, hiking, watching movies, and reading. Being present is my challenge. I've learned (in some cases the hard way!) not to multitask when I am visiting with my children and grandchildren. Whether I am engaged in a phone conversation or Face Timing, I have learned to stop everything else and focus on them and the context of the conversation.

My children would much rather have 15 minutes of uninterrupted time than half of my focus for 30. I haven't mastered this skill yet, but I am seeing tremendous results. Now, instead of my being the one to say I have to go, they say it! I have seen an amazing turn-around in our relationships, and I have discovered the power of being fully present has brought us that much closer.

I have also learned a valuable insight about the importance of *grace*. As I began to grow and become more aware of how to be a better parent, I was able to see my own parents through a new lens. I have learned to give my own parents a break. They did the best they could with what they knew at that time. I have learned to take what I liked about the way they raised me, and I have emulated that in my own parenting. The other principles I decided to ditch. I have learned to love my parents for what they did right. I have found this new view to be freeing, which is why I feel compelled to share these insights.

EXTENDED FAMILY

We were designed to be part of a family. We were designed to function as a family, to learn love, passion, boundaries, rules, consequences, and rewards within this context. Admittedly, family has been a tricky and touchy subject for me. I have been involved in relationships that have ebbed and flowed over many years.

I am part of a blended family. Like I mentioned earlier, I am the eldest of four children. When my mom remarried I gained five stepbrothers. One of them was 5 months older than I which left 7 more children under age 10. My mom gets serious kudos for not ever having the need to enter an insane asylum. The good news was that I got to beat up on those younger siblings for awhile and move out before they were ever bigger than me and could return the favor. The bad news is that some of us aren't very close.

I suppose our family would be classified as "dysfunctional." I have often pondered if any families ever really function well. In my experience in talking with people, I have learned that every family has dirt and skeletons. I have also learned by my experience and in learning from others, that the hurts and mistakes we make as individuals and as members of a family, can serve as positive learning experiences. With the right attitude, counseling, and introspection, these experiences can serve as functional learning strategies for the future.

I'd like to share a couple of stories/examples of lessons I've learned in my family.

Sometimes these relationships are hard. Sometimes in order to protect yourself and your family, you have to distance yourself from a relationship in the name of peace and protection of sanity. I have an extended family member who thrives on drama. We are talking about screaming at the top your lungs, hateful, mean disregard for others feelings kind of drama. But this person is a part of my family and I need to try and maintain some semblance of a relationship, right? I need to forgive and forget, accept her for who she is, and try, try again?

In my case, I'm sad to say the answer to that question is a resounding no. Attempting to salvage the relationship repeatedly, to be around the immediate vicinity of drama, and find myself on the backlash end of any type of confrontation that came down was exhausting, hurtful, and damaging to my other relationships within my family. In the end, I completely and totally forgave that person (as you know the only one hurt by not forgiving someone is yourself) and had to cut all ties to that person.

I had followed the same routine for decades. The relative would make peace, try and be sweet for awhile until the inevitable massive blow-up happened leaving our relationship in shreds. Time would pass and we would start all over again. The thing is, I really feel sorry for this relative. She needs help. She suffered a divorce, was left with a gaggle of kids, and is in need of all sorts of support. But in the end, that person drove ALL of her relatives away.

My best wishes and blessings go out to her, but I had to stop the broken record of our relationship and let myself mend. I truly hope that someday we can start again for real this time. But in the meantime, for the peace, serenity, and protection of myself and my family, I've had to cut all ties. This is of course always true in the cases of physical or verbal abuse. If you find yourself in this position, seek help now. Remember the Maya Angelou quote that says, "When people show you who they are, believe them the first time."

In contrast to this experience, there is my husband's family. At first I didn't even know what to do with them. They are completely drama free. Seriously! Now it may be to the fault of not talking about things when they need to sometimes, but I love and appreciate their example.

They are 100% devoted to each other both in their immediate and extended families. My family is really active, not only laughing out loud, playing out loud, being boisterous in a good way and not without our share of drama from time to time, but not Eddy's family. They are rock solid, caring, and considerate of each other. If you have a family like this, you are truly blessed! Be eternally grateful for their example and their love always.

I love my mom. I put her through hell as a teenager and young adult for a lot of years. Too many to count. Our relationship has been one of ebb and flow. Currently we are in a flow so that's good! Unfortunately, my mom got sucked into that drama vampire I talked about a minute ago in our family. She was a true saint as far as I'm concerned. She helped that relative right alongside my dad for about 17 years before my mom's line was finally crossed and she couldn't help anymore either. Due to that toxic relationship, my relationship with my mom took a turn for the worse.

While my mom and I do not always see eye to eye, she is the relative that I want in my life, have fun with, and even ask advice from when I need it the most. She would do anything for me. If I call and need help, she is there almost immediately.

I have learned, in the name of self-preservation, sometimes cutting ties with people is the most healthy action to take. This might not be forever, but perfectly ok to protect yourself from hurt and unnecessary drama. If you have a family like my in-laws, don't feel like you're bored - embrace them and love them for all they're worth! If you can, foster the relationship with your parents. If that relationship is toxic and you're not the cause of toxicity, I understand the need for distance. If on the other hand you can think of a way to bridge the gap, please do something today to mend that relationship. By small and simple things are great things brought to pass. This is an eye-opening truth in our extended family relationships.

FRIENDS

Sitting in church one day, my friend Lori and I were complaining about how we didn't know a lot of people in our church family. No one had hurt our feelings or purposefully shunned us, we just didn't feel a part. After thinking on this for awhile, I realized that we had no one to blame but ourselves. We decided that we would take the quote to heart and BE a friend.

So what did we do? We made a list of 10 getting to know you questions, sat in the very back of church that next Sunday and picked out someone we didn't know well. We then contacted that woman and asked if she had any free time that week. When we met with our "new friend," we sat with them, told them how we felt, what we were doing, and that we wanted to get to know them better.

The most amazing thing happened. That very next week we had a new friend. And the Lori/Lauri project was born. I was blessed to make many new friends in our church family and while not all of us became "besties" we did manage to get ourselves out of our friendship slump.

To have a friend, you have to be a friend. Maybe you're a person who keeps one close friend. Maybe you have a handful of closer friends. Or perhaps you're the social butterfly that needs a group of friends that all hang together. Whatever your cup of tea with friends happens to be - please love and enjoy your friends.

If you are in need of finding new friends, may I suggest the Lori/Lauri Project? Synchronicity will step in as you put forth the effort and friends will "magically" appear.

CHURCH

If you are fortunate enough to be a part of a faith-based community family - congratulations! Having a firm faith belief in whatever practice you choose can be an integral part of how you view the world. There is a great opportunity for positivity in these organizations.

I was raised in a faith-based community, but didn't find my true conviction until well into my adult years. It has left such a mark on me that I am devoting an entire book to that journey and so will only touch lightly on it in this section.

If you recall from my romantic relationship section, I stunk at being married and after my third one was excommunicated. Not only did my family and friends see the error of my ways and tried to warn me (it's always hardest to see it when you're in the middle of it), but my clergy warned me of my foolishness. I let my pride get in the way and ignored advice from everyone.

I have decided to give a preview of another story into my life: How it felt to be excommunicated. Here is an excerpt from the first chapter of the book I will write next:

"The knock at the door was almost anticipated and yet the

dread I felt when answering was nothing compared to the
emptiness that would in the next few minutes consume me.
My thoughts, my actions, my rebellious pride had brought me
to this place. This moment where time itself would seem to
stand still and my life felt as if it were hanging in the balance.
I received the letter without anything more than a curt thank
you as the two members of the Bishopric left and the door
closed. My feet felt like blocks of cement and I was rooted to
the floor. After a brief hesitation, the letter was ever so slowly
opened and I took a short breath before reading the contents
of what I already knew. Dropping to the floor as I read, barely
able to see the words through the hot tears already rolling
down my face, feeling the sudden emptiness of losing my
most precious gift that I had not guarded well hit me with the
force of a flash flood through desert canyons, taking with it
everything in its path. I had been excommunicated."

As you can see, I was devastated. I tell you this not so you
feel sorry for me, but to illustrate a point. I had a choice right
then and there. One, tell them to piss off and do whatever the
heck I wanted to, or two, decide what I really believed: did I
want to return to full fellowship in my church?; could I fight
and claw my way back with *patience*? That's what I did, I
learned patience.

I learned that church is not an institution for perfect people,
but rather, it's a hospital for the sick at heart. I learned that I
believed in God, in Jesus Christ, and in the Holy Ghost. I
learned that what my stepdad said was true, "I looked at all of
the churches, and found that this one most closely aligned
with my beliefs so I'm throwing my hat in the ring with
them." I learned that my church believes strongly in family
and community. That they set a good precedent between right
and wrong as well as teaching not just honesty, but integrity. I

learned how to let others help me on my journey and that I didn't have to figure life out alone. Basically, I learned about a belief system that I can stand behind and defend, and I also learned that love, faith, and patience were necessary traits to have if I was going to pursue a life of happiness and contribute positivity to the world.

To get back to re-baptism, I had to work hard to change. I learned the value of trusting God, listening to Him, and learning to love myself and others in a healthy way. I had been making poor decisions for a long time and I had much to learn, so several years passed before I was back in full fellowship of the church. I learned how to apply patience and waiting to my circumstances. I learned that these traits lead to positive outcomes.

I encourage you to become deeply involved if you are part of a faith-based community. Nurturing yourself within this kind of loving community will help you grow in ways you never expected. Taking part in activities, hanging out with the people you enjoy, and participating in service will bring new experiences and fun in your life! If church just isn't your thing, please disregard this entire section. I love you either way.

WORK

As humans, we were designed to work and serve. Our attitudes about our jobs are usually a direct reflection of our internal thoughts and perspectives. Think about the times where you have encountered people who love their jobs. They smile. They flourish in their environment. Their energy is contagious! Sadly, I've seen time and time again people who have complained about their jobs and laid blame to everyone but themselves. I can't help but wonder if they changed their attitude, if their environment might change too? I have seen cases where this does happen and the person has saved his job. You might be thinking, how can I alter my way of seeing my job?

Disclaimer: If you change your view and attitude about your job and your boss or co-worker is still a bully or abusive in any way - you may need to re-think your current job situation.

For example, I have an ex-husband who once had 5 jobs in one year. He was insistent that his moving from one job to the next didn't have anything to do with him. How is that possible? The only common denominator in the all of these scenarios was him. I have another relative who has the same issue. The job starts out great, then she takes time off because of a personal issue that her boss "doesn't understand." In the end, the company has zero reason to keep them on board and lets them go. Again, the these types of people see the company or the boss as the bad guy and they take zero responsibility for their own actions and attitudes. Don't let this be you!

If you want to quit, quit. But don't blame everyone else and have a pity party, even if it's a catered pity party. Own your sh**. BUT, you might be thinking, how can I change my attitude at work? How can I make peace in the workplace so I can do my job to the best of my ability? I encourage you to try this exercise. It's only two steps. You got this!

First, ask yourself this question: "What do I love about my job?" Write all the reasons you can think of. Maybe you started because the company had a great reputation and they are out to save the world one pair of socks at a time, like

Bombas. Maybe it's for the great incentive of a paycheck every two weeks! I like the paycheck part myself. Maybe it's because your office has a view or the company picks up the tab for your membership to your local gym. Write them all down.

Second, find one thing every day that you can compliment someone on at work. If this isn't your habit or routine, this is going to be hard at first. What makes offering someone a compliment easier is the compliment doesn't have to have anything to do with their job performance. Nothing. It can be as simple as "I like what you did with your hair today" or "nice shoes, where did you get them?"

Do both of these things, reading your list daily, adding to when needed, and complimenting someone at work for the next two weeks and see if anything changes. One thing will happen for sure - you will change.

After all of the other social relationships we've talked about, I put our neighborhoods and communities and the fact that it's ok to say no to energy and time vampires at the end of our list.

I'm betting that if you've made it this far into the book and have stayed open-minded, that you've done some serious soul-searching and maybe even faced yourself in the mirror with bravery and honesty, that you're now ready to take what you've learned and find the best version of you within the 30-Day Power of Positivity Challenge just waiting on the next page. Here we go!

30-DAY POWER OF POSITIVITY
CHALLENGE

Welcome and thank you for being a part of this fun and rewarding 30-Day Power of Positivity Challenge!

Here at Lauri's Lemonade Stand, we practice The Art of Holiatry (hoh-lee-a-tree) which is meant to create a holistic approach to healing and living life to the fullest. To find balance. The Holiatry Triangle (pictured here) shows that you are at the center of this triangle. You are the seed planted right smack dab in the middle. You will pull from the ground where you are planted by nourishing your physical and psychological self - this is where you learn and grow. Once you achieve this balance, you are ready to bloom into the Social triangle where you find out how to show up in the world, how to show up in your relationships.

Fun Fact: Symbolism of the Holiatry Triangle

There is significance to every part of this symbol. I created it specifically to speak to every part of you. The whole you.

Let's start with the colors!

Purple is the color for the entirety of Holiatry. Purple is associated with wisdom, dignity, independence, creativity, mystery, and magic.

Blue symbolizes you. Trust, loyalty, wisdom, confidence, intelligence, faith, truth, and heaven.

Yellow represents the Physical triangle of Holiatry. Yellow is associated with joy, happiness, intellect, and energy. It stimulates muscle energy.

Orange represents the Psychological triangle of Holiatry. Orange is associated with enthusiasm, fascination, happiness, creativity, determination, attraction, success, encouragement, and stimulation.

Green represents the Social triangle of Holiatry. Green has great healing power. It symbolizes growth, harmony, freshness, and hope.

The font and flowers!

The daisies symbolize innocence and purity. In Norse mythology, the daisy is Freya's sacred flower. Freya is the goddess of love, beauty, and fertility, and as such the daisy has come to symbolize childbirth, motherhood, and new beginnings. It is this new beginnings that I am looking for in these next 30 days of positivity.

The font was Celtic in nature to honor the meaning and history of the daisies.

Every 10 days over the next 30 we will focus on each of these triangles. The first 10 days will spotlight the Physical Triangle (nourishment and movement). The second 10 days will highlight The Psychological Triangle (mind & spirit). The last 10 days will target the Social Triangle where you will learn some new ideas about all sorts of relationships from strangers to your love partners and even to work.

Every day will have a quote to contemplate and meditate on (or just make you smile), a short description of the day, your daily challenge, and if you're like me and love music, a daily song to inspire you or just make you want to move and dance! If you want to do "extra credit", I've also left you a daily resource to check out with some of my favorite cookbooks, books, websites, blogs, you name it. The resources are not a requirement, just me sharing a few of my favorite things with you in case something strikes your fancy.

DISCLOSURE: The nutritional content in this challenge is designed for informational purposes only and should not be used in any other manner. The information found here should not serve as a substitute for medical advice. Your personal physician should review any and all diet, wellness, and exercise programs before you begin. Please consult a medical professional with your health concerns or conditions, and practice careful consideration before following any method to treat mental, emotional, or physical illness - no matter the source.

PHYSICAL: NOURISHMENT/MOVEMENT/REST

The first 10 days of your 30 Day Power of Positivity Challenge will begin with your physical body.

How do you nourish your body? What type of fuel are you using? Is it full of nutrients or devoid of nutrients? Days 1-5 will focus directly on this beautiful nourishment for the inside and outside of our bodies and some ways to add in more healthy foods into your menu.

Days 6-10 focuses on the movement and needed rest for your body. What is your favorite movement? Do you like to ride your bicycle? Do you prefer to dance? Maybe it's surfing or walking or kick-boxing? What turns you on in this department? What lights you up when you think about doing it? We will focus on creating movement and getting enough sleep in so that we can then focus on our mind & spirit in our next 10 days of Psychological.

Day 1:

Daily Quote: "Remember, what you consume (both nutritionally and energetically) is the fuel of your life." - Kristi Ling

Personal Insight: Sometimes just thinking about something, becoming aware of your thoughts or actions is enough to inspire change. Today's quote by Kristi Ling, author of *Operation Happiness* asks us to simply remember that what we consume as fuel and how we expend that fuel can quite literally make us happy. Because this is Day 1, we will start out with a simple challenge. Enjoy!

Daily Challenge: Buy your favorite fruit or vegetable and make a meal surrounding it. For example, have broccoli be the main dish and everything else on your plate will simply be side dishes to the main event of the broccoli. If you prefer fruit as your main dish, try surrounding it with raw nuts, nut butters, or vegan artisan cashew cheese.

Daily Song Recommendation: "Best Day of My Life" by American Authors

There is a line in this song that says "all the possibilities, no limits just epiphanies" that makes me smile every time. This song is upbeat, fun, and a great way to start off the first day of our 30-Day Power of Positivity Challenge. Feel free to have your own little dance party while listening!

Daily Resource: Every once in awhile you come across a cookbook with a chef that just nails the combination of flavors in every. single. recipe. The Abundance Diet by Somer McCowan is my all-time favorite cookbook and you can grab it right here on Amazon: http://amzn.to/2ql7GyN (Tip: When making the cashew sour cream, eliminate the dry mustard and definitely use a vegan probiotic - it makes all the difference in this particular recipe.)

Day 2:

Daily Quote: "Change can be hard at first, messy in the middle, and gorgeous in the end." - Robin Sharma

Personal Insight: I've worn many hats in my lifetime and believe it or not I dabbled in being a professional organizer for a bit. My tagline was "to clean a mess, you have to make a mess". Think about it. What happens when you clean out your closet? You're yanking stuff out, trying things on, dumping things, cleaning out the cobwebs and vacuuming under your shoe racks. It's hard at first, messy in the middle, but gorgeous in the end.

The same holds true for anything we are trying to clean up in our lives and because we are focusing on our diet for these first five days, let's mix things up a bit and turn it on it's head!

Daily Challenge: Eat breakfast for dinner! Sometimes it's hard to change only because we are stuck in a rut. Embracing change, as it is the only thing that ever stays the same by the way, helps us to change our perspective. This can be most helpful in changing our diets. Add an element of fun as Mary Poppins so famously said to any job that must be done. Enjoy this waffle recipe that I prepare every single Sunday for lunch!

Ch, Ch, Ch, Chia Waffles

4 ripe medium bananas

5 Tbsp chia seeds

4 over-filled cups of regular oats

4 tsp no-alcohol vanilla

3 tsp ground cinnamon

2 cups unsweetened almond milk

In a food processor, drop the bananas in chunks and then blend a bit before adding chia seeds and blending a bit more just so the chia seeds are wet. Set timer for 10 minutes. While timer is running, add remaining ingredients and just pulse until blended, but so that the oats are not pulverized. Let sit until timer goes off. Spread evenly in your waffle iron and cook for 9 minutes. Tip: they will not be done when the light goes off on your waffle maker. They need the full 9 minutes.

In fact, I put my second batch and any remaining batches in for 12 minutes each.

Top with nut butters (my favorites are Laura Scudders creamy peanut butter and Trader Joe's brand unsalted chunky almond butter) with fresh fruit or jam.

Daily Song Recommendation: "Change In The Making" by Mercy River

"There's a better version of me, That I can't quite see, But things are gonna change" This song epitomizes that change is possible.

Daily Resource: Confession time! I am a die-hard vegan and have been whole foods, plant-based for over 5 years as of the making of this challenge and promote it like crazy! And I don't eat sugar. Any kind of sugar. If you need a break from sugar, I will direct you to Samantha Russell's freebie on her website entitled, "7-Day Sugar Detox Journaling Challenge". It works and it can be done! Check it out by clicking here: http://livethewhole.com/7-day-sugar-detox-journal-challenge/

Extra Credit: Download and listen to Sam's Interview on Lauri's Lemonade Stand Podcast, episode #058!

Day 3:

Daily Quote: "As I improved my diet, I started to learn to love myself, probably for the first time ever." - Frank Ferrante

Personal Insight: The scariest part about going vegan was what on earth I was going to cook for me and my family. Now, while you might not embrace this type of diet, you will probably agree that everyone could benefit from adding more fruits and vegetables in their meal planning, right? There are more resources than ever out there these days, but vegan can be done incredibly unhealthfully. A good example of this is that Coca-Cola, Pepsi, potato chips, french fries and Oreos are all vegan. Just because they are vegan does not make them healthy.

This is why I embrace what is called a whole foods, plant-based diet. It eliminates processed foods, all oils (the most highly concentrated form of fat on the planet and most definitely processed), and keeps me fueling my body the best way I know how. But like I said…in the beginning I had no idea how or what to cook so I got educated. So educated that I started taking cooking classes, buying cookbooks, and became a Certified Holistic Health Coach with a certificate in plant-based nutrition. I now teach vegan cooking classes to others!

Daily Challenge: Today's challenge is to go vegan for one day. Include a breakfast, lunch, afternoon snack, and dinner. The resource below will help you find recipes unless you ordered the resource from Day 1, have Amazon Prime and Somer's cookbook is arriving today! :) If you are reading this and it just seems to overwhelming to accomplish right this moment, simply make the grocery list, go shopping today, and embrace your vegan side tomorrow. It's all good. Win the Day!

Daily Song Recommendation: "Win The Day" by Hilary Weeks

"Let your faith be bigger than your fears, stay strong, never give up" Pay special attention to the words of this song… uplifting and motivating to quite literally Win The Day!

Daily Resource: The movie, Forks Over Knives now on

Netflix! If you don't have Netflix (I don't!), then you can buy it on Amazon here: http://amzn.to/2rGRqfB This is a cautionary documentary from two men who grew up on dairy farms and one becomes a research scientist, and one a heart surgeon. Their discoveries about protein, heart disease, and cancer will have you re-thinking your diet and feeling better in no time.

Not a movie watcher? Just enjoy some delicious whole food, plant-based nutrition recipes here: ForksOverKnives.com/recipes There are so many to choose from that you could make weeks of menus from this list!

Want to go deeper with the food? Take the Forks over Knives Cooking Class by clicking here: https://www.forksoverknives.com/cooking-course/#gs.3R4k8iw Whether you're just making the transition to a plant-based diet, or want to learn how to expand your skills in the kitchen, this is the plant-based online cooking course for you. When you click on the link in this paragraph there are some sample videos to see what you're getting into, but I've heard nothing but positive feedback on this course.

Day 4:

Daily Quote: "Women have fought so long and hard for our rights and equality, and now all our attention is put on being a size 0." - Pink

Personal Insight: Embracing my Gray? or Celebrating my Silver? I choose to celebrate my silver! I choose to ignore corporate expectations in ads from billboards to magazines to television and celebrate my silver, get excited about my freckles and my bike tan that keeps my hands white from wearing gloves while I ride and shows a sock tan when I wear dresses to church. I LOVE MY LIFE! I am strong. I am beautiful. And so are you.

While nourishment on the inside is good and we need to pay attention to what we put *inside* our body, it is also just as important to be aware of what we put *on* our body. Learn about the ingredients in your body care products and simply make yourself more aware of what you are consuming through your skin.

Daily Challenge: Mirror Work. You can learn to love your life and embrace your life. Mirror work offers you a moment to look yourself in the eye and tell yourself that you are strong, that you are worthy of love, that you are beautiful. Pick one of the three phrases below, stand in front of the mirror and with conviction and love say them to yourself 5 times. You might feel foolish at first, but this is a genuine practice to LOVE YOUR LIFE!

"I am strong. I fight for what I believe to be right."

"I truly believe that I am beautiful. Beauty is my super-power."

"I am loved. I am worthy of love. I give love in abundance."

Daily Song Recommendation: "Love Your Life" by Hilary Weeks

"Go beyond your fears, explore new ground, be true to yourself, and when in doubt, listen to your heart as it whispers where you need to go and always look up." Being true to yourself isn't always easy, but it's worth it. Let this song in, through, and around you. Embrace the lyrics and see how they might apply to you in navigating your own set of "crazy twists and turns."

Daily Resource: Boom! by Cindy Joseph.
https://www.boombycindyjoseph.com/

Introducing the first Pro-Age cosmetic line for women of every generation. Cindy Joseph, make-up artist turned super model, has created a line of cosmetics just for you. BOOM! is for women who want to reveal their genuine beauty with an honest and realistic approach.

Confession: I don't wear make-up. I have eyelash extensions put on every 3 weeks, my eyeliner is tattooed on, my eyebrows and upper lip no longer have unwanted hair because I had the unwanted ones permanently removed using thermolysis, and I only use Cindy's products. 3 products and that's it! Done…time saved in the bathroom every day. It's worth checking into!

Extra Credit: Listen to Cindy Joseph's interview on Lauri's Lemonade Stand Podcast episode #030!

Day 5:

Daily Quote: "Happiness is a skill." - Kristi Ling

Personal Insight: I would be remiss if I didn't bring up the fact that some of us have issues around food. I will just start by telling you that I struggle with food addiction. I have a problem surrounding food obsession and scale obsession. The only thing that set me free was deciding to attend a 12-step meeting and finding Bright Line Eating by Susan Peirce Thompson, PhD. I gave up sugar and flour, I eat 3 meals a day and while I am not "cured" I wanted to address the elephant in the room because it's ok to admit if you have a problem. How do you know if you have a problem around food? Take today's challenge and find out! Be Brave!

Daily Challenge: Are you addicted to food? Learn whether your BRAIN is BLOCKING you from losing weight. Foods today are highly addictive, but not everyone is equally affected. Discovering your susceptibility to addictive foods is the first step to getting Happy, Thin, and Free. How susceptible are you? Take the Food Susceptibility Quiz by clicking here: foodfreedomquiz.com.

Daily Song Recommendation: "Brave" by Hilary Weeks

"You are brave, let your brave come through, let it define you, you are meant to brave. You're about to see a you you've never seen before." I know you're hearing quite a few days of Hilary Weeks and I promise it will be mixed up a bit in the days to come, but her words ring true to my heart and I just had to share them with you.

Daily Resource: brightlineeating.com by Susan Peirce Thompson, PhD. "Happy, Thin, and Free" is what Susan promises by following her food plan. You can go to her website to buy her book, sign up for a boot camp, or simply sign up to receive her Wednesday VLOG's that are always FREE!

Extra Credit: Listen to Susan Peirce Thompson's interview on Lauri's Lemonade Stand Podcast episode #020!

Day 6:

Daily Quote: "Exercise to stimulate, not to annihilate. The world wasn't formed in a day and neither were we. Set small goals and build upon them." - Lee Haney

Personal Insight: Baby Steps. We do ourselves a disservice by biting off more than we can chew. Personally, there are only a few things that need to not take baby steps. Addiction is one of them…it is better to go cold turkey and fast. Quitting any type of addiction is better served this way. But most things require baby steps and in the long run are more effective in sticking to your commitments.

I feel it is best to first form a consistent habit. Let's take a for instance…

What if you want to run a 5k? That doesn't mean that you go out, run every day for a week and then you're ready. It means setting a schedule at either 2 or 3 days per week, downloading a couch to 5k app, and starting a walking/jogging program over the course of the next 2-3 months. The key to success here is to be consistent. Choose 2 or 3 days per week with very specific times that you are going to practice no matter what.

It is far more important to show up and do something, then fall off the wagon and say "I don't feel like it today." I would even go as far as talking about the weather. "I'm going to walk/jog rain or shine, even if I don't feel well or up to it." (The only exception to this is if you have some kind of head cold…then I recommend letting that clear up first. Otherwise, you risk getting a sinus infection or getting something dreadful like pneumonia or bronchitis.)

Another example would be something as simple as doing 100 sit-ups per night, M-F. It is far better to get on the floor and try every single night then to commit to 5 days a week, only do 2 days and then quit altogether. Baby Steps.

Daily Challenge: Walking is the best form of universal exercise. It accomplishes so much! It gets you out of the house, into nature, makes you move your body, and as in today's challenge, lets you listen to some fun music! Please purchase and download Erin Stutland's Soul Stroll here: https://shrinksession.com/soul-stroll-1/

Daily Song Recommendation: "Soul Stroll" by Erin Stutland (Link Above & Below)

Erin has two Soul Strolls available for you and they are amazing! A pick-me-up and empowerment of self all in one. Erin takes upbeat music and combines it with positive affirmations that will leave you feeling uplifted and ready to conquer anything! (Even if taking baby steps to do it!)

https://shrinksession.com/soul-stroll-1/

https://shrinksession.com/soul-stroll-2/

Daily Resource: ShrinkSessionWorkout.com by Erin Stutland. If you want to get a Soul Stroll for free, just purchase Erin's Shrink Session Workout here: https://shrinksession.com/shrinksession/. Each Shrink Session is a mix of cardio-dance, yoga, and kickboxing that makes double use of the time you dedicate to working out. The movements elevate your heart rate and tone your body while the mantras (positive affirmations) elevate your thinking.

Day 7:

Daily Quote: "Although beauty may be in the eye of the beholder, the feeling of being beautiful exists solely in the mind of the beheld." - Martha Beck

Personal Insight: What is it about yoga that makes me feel fluid and beautiful? At peace with the outside world and more importantly, the inside world? Yoga is sexy. When it comes to being mindful, I find it best when practicing yoga.

I'm also well over 40 and feel sexy when I use my muscles! I am not a body-builder, but I like a little more lift on my biceps and less sag on my triceps. :) Hence, today's challenge and resource for you to jump on this bandwagon and have you feeling sexy in no time! (Well, not no time...you will have to dedicate some time here, but you get the gist.)

Daily Challenge: Take a yoga class. If you are a member of a local club or gym, try it. Look up a local yoga studio and try that. Or download the Gaiam yoga app for less than what it would cost in person. Or just try a free one on YouTube. The benefit would be to go to today's resource and use the yoga/strength-training videos that wrap it all in one - a one-stop shop of balance, yoga, strength-training, and flexibility!

Daily Song Recommendation: "Feel the Love" by Cahill & Kimberley Locke

"Put your fears aside, let your troubles go...Feel the Love" This song is upbeat and makes me want to dance around my living room. I invite you to Feel The Love with Kimberley Locke's amazing voice!

Daily Resource: With Sadie Nardini's HIIT (High Intensity Interval Training) Yoga, you get to find peace while still embracing the Lady Gaga, freak, rock-n-roll side of you. Simply go to http://sadienardini.com/ and download her app or sign up for a class today. She is amazing!

Extra Credit: Listen to Kimberley Locke's interview on Lauri's Lemonade Stand Podcast episode #047 and Sadie Nardini's interview episode #076!

Day 8:

Daily Quote: "If we could give every individual the right amount of nourishment and exercise, not too little and not too much, we would have found the safest way to health." - Hippocrates

Personal Insight: Last year I hired a cycling coach for four months. Basically, I became a bad-ass mountain biker which was one of my goals. I was making it up technical climbs and hills that I had never been able to conquer before - I made it! The problem was that the rest of my body felt completely out of balance. My biceps and triceps suffered and I was eating everything in sight because I was working out like a fiend and gained 10 pounds. While my feats of strength were impressive, even to me - I had to acknowledge that I was out of balance for what rang true to me.

I then decided to focus on what that "balance" meant for me. Like Hippocrates stated in the quote above, "just the right amount" is the safest way to MY health. Not anyone else's, but mine. I have found balance in my movement routine. But sometimes we get bored with our routines, right?

I have a personal trainer friend (we all have at least one, right?) who was hosting a 4-week bootcamp at the beginning of summer and I jumped on board! I believe it's good to mix it up and challenge ourselves, but 2 weeks in I was eating a ton of food again and was a bit out of balance - for me.

I've learned to listen to my body, still be a pretty kick-ass mountain biking Gramma, an amateur yoga student who can run 5k's and still pull off a road-bike ride up to 50 miles without killing myself. Throw in a couple of small gym workouts during the week to keep it toned up and my body loves me and I'm loving my body!

Daily Challenge: Download an exercise app and use it today. It could be the free 7-minute butt workout or 7-minute arm workout. Perhaps it's a yoga app (Gaiam Yoga Studio is my favorite) or maybe you want to up your game and go for the Couch to 5k app by Active or if you're further along, the 5k to 10k app also by Active. Choose something and go for it! What is calling you?

Daily Song Recommendation: "Born This Way" by Lady Gaga

"Rejoice and love yourself today, cause baby you were born this way!"

Daily Resource: I've only used Victoria's Secret Yoga pants for years. Whether you are the perfect model or are like me and have birthed three kids and need a little bit of holding in and holding up, these have never failed me. I run in them, yoga in them, gym in them, and even have one pair that I now paint walls in (don't ask…it's a long story). Check out their leggings by clicking here: http://bit.ly/2fCY1CS

Day 9:

Daily Quote: "Standards of beauty are arbitrary. Body shame exists only to the extent that our physiques don't match our own beliefs about how we should look." - Martha Beck

Personal Insight: We are our own worst critics. No one can tell us something that we haven't already harped on ourselves about. If I were to ask you right now what you would change about your body, I'd bet you'd have a laundry list at the ready and it would be prioritized on what you would change first.

How have we programmed ourselves to think like this? I do this constantly and to the point where I literally ended up on my bathroom floor in a heap and in tears because I hated my body. I don't want to be like that anymore! I want to love my body…right here. Right NOW!!

While I am not proficient at this yet, but I give myself a break considering I've lived my entire life thinking of my faults and have only recently started learning how to love every single part of myself. It might take time, but I'm working on it. Today's Challenge will leave you feeling liberated and today's Daily Resource will quite literally have you screaming, "I LOVE MY BODY!"

Daily Challenge: Throw away your bathroom scale.

Daily Song Recommendation: "Shatter Me" by Lindsey Stirling

Watch the video version of this song so that you see the concept of breaking free. PS - This is the song I listen to when I'm bombing downhill on my mountain bike! Love it! You can watch it here: https://bit.ly/1jDtJWb

Daily Resource: Embrace Movie by Taryn Brumfitt (Watch Trailer here: https://bodyimagemovement.com/embrace/about-the-film/)

"EMBRACE is a social impact documentary that explores the issue of body image. The project has been supported by nearly 9000 Kickstarter pledgers who responded to a fundraising trailer I released in 2014, which has now had over 25 million internet views.

"The inspiration for EMBRACE came about after I posted an unconventional before-and-after image on the internet in

2013 that sparked an international media frenzy. The image, which embraces body diversity, was seen by over 100 million people worldwide and led to hundreds of interviews and articles. But I soon realized how restrictive 4-minute TV interviews, 800 word articles and 140 characters on Twitter can be. This issue needed a louder voice on a bigger platform, so the idea of creating the documentary EMBRACE was born." – Embrace Director Taryn Brumfitt

Embrace is told from the point of view of Taryn as she traverses the globe talking to experts, women in the street and well-known personalities about the alarming rates of body image issues that are seen in people of all body types. In her affable and effervescent style, Taryn bares all (literally) to explore the factors contributing to this problem and seeks to find solutions.

After 24 months of travelling, interviewing, production and post production Taryn and the Embrace team have created a film that is relevant, relatable, highly engaging – but above all life changing.

Embrace had its world premiere at the 2016 Sydney Film Festival, where it made it into the festival directors' top 5 picks and was nominated for the Documentary Australia Foundation Award for Best Documentary.

Day 10:

Daily Quote: "Practice puts brains in your muscles."
-Sam Snead

Personal Insight: Wouldn't it be great if we could just work out every day for 30 days and have it last the rest of the year? Or practice a musical instrument non-stop for the same amount of time and be proficient the rest of the time? Once it's learned it's learned? Practice will never make perfect, but practice does make permanent. Practice makes habits permanent.

Much like what I talked about in Day 6 in taking baby steps and being consistent, we need to practice to make our habit permanent. I'm not saying that we'll nail it each and every day, but "practice puts brains in your muscles".

Daily Challenge: Create a workout playlist. On my phone and iPod I have numerous playlists. Motivate, Melancholy, Smile, Time to Sing, and three workout playlists...Bike, Run, and Gym. Some of the songs overlap and I've been adding new songs for years so it's pretty eclectic. I even have the Shazam app on my phone and bust it out during movies, in restaurants, in the car if the radio happens to be on, in the mall, and sometimes just watching YouTube videos of killer mountain bikers! Put on that music and as Diana Ross says, "I'm Coming Out, I want the world to know, gonna let is show!"

Daily Song Recommendation: "I'm Coming Out" by Diana Ross

Daily Resource: Music moves me. It helps me to stay calm, get motivated, soothe me when I'm melancholy, and I show you here - gets me moving when I work out! Check out this link to my blog (don't forget to leave me a comment when you've read it!) and check out every song I have on my playlist for cycling! This is especially helpful when I'm mountain biking! Enjoy! http://bit.ly/2s4CvMT

PSYCHOLOGICAL: MIND/SPIRIT/SELF-LOVE

One of my favorite parts about the Art of Holiatry is how everything is intertwined. Holistic means the sum of your parts, not just the parts. We are looking at the WHOLE SYNERGY of you, not just the parts. Now, while we are working on certain parts of our triangle specifically, can you see how they are intertwined and helping the overall WHOLE of YOU? It is a beautiful symphony where all the parts are needed to make the best of music. Wait until you see what's in store for you over these second 10 days that are based on your mind & spirit!

Day 11:

Daily Quote: "Action may not always bring happiness, but there is no happiness without action." - Benjamin Disraeli, former British Prime Minister

Personal Insight: Do you ever hear or say, "I just can't get motivated" or "I'm waiting to get motivated"? I'm here to toss this belief right out the window and tell you that motivation is Step 2, not Step 1.

There are a total of 4 steps to get moving in the direction of your dreams. I'm not talking about just big dreams like buying a house or writing a book either. These 4 steps will work if you can't get motivated to clean out your closet or your garage. Here's how it works:

Step 1 - Action

Actions can be big or small, an idea, a baby step, or jumping off a cliff...whatever it is, you do you. What is your why? How will you feel once you've accomplished your goal? How will you feel once you take some time to plan it out or take that first baby step towards accomplishing it?

When I decided to graduate high school as an adult (Took my GED after 10th grade...still wanted my diploma) the first step was not waiting to get motivated. If I had waited, I would still be waiting. I made a plan, I met with a counselor, figured out how many credits I needed and tackled it class by crazy class. What is your why and your baby step that you can take towards it?

Step 2 - Motivation

Motivation happens AFTER you take that first step. You make the plan, take the class, buy new exercise clothes, get an accountability partner, hire the personal trainer...whatever it is! There is nothing that motivates me more to work out than buying new workout clothes...I know, I know, but that's what does it for me! What does it for you?

Step 3 - Momentum

The key to reaching your goal is then momentum or what I like to call sticktoitiveness. You take an action step, it creates motivation, you take another action step, it creates more motivation and then you've created Momentum. You - you created it! Keep it going sister, and then move to the final step 4.

Step 4 - Celebrate!

This is an imperative step. Sounds crazy, right? We NEED to celebrate our wins, our victories, our best efforts! I'm not saying you will succeed at everything and sometimes you will be called upon to celebrate your failures so you can move past something, but celebrating is an imperative step to keeping that momentum moving! Celebrate the small wins and the big ones (or even the failures)…they all deserve your time and attention.

Daily Challenge: Today I will take the baby action step of

_____.

Remember that this can be anywhere from writing down your plan to setting a date to do something, but make sure it's an action step in the direction you want to go!

Daily Song Recommendation: "Rock Bottom" by Wynonna Judd

I love this song! It talks about hitting rock bottom and how tough that can be. "When you get down to nothin', you got nothin' to lose!" "A dead end street is just a place to turn around." Get up, dance or sing to this song as your action step…it will surely lead to motivation!

Daily Resource: There are times when you're just going to feel blocked in the direction of your dreams. This is where I recommend spending some time journaling. My friend, Laurie Blackwell is an expert at journaling! She has fun classes, a free monthly handwritten newsletter and other freebies to help you on your way. Find her here: http://www.laurieblackwell.com

Extra Credit: Listen to Laurie Blackwell's interview on Lauri's Lemonade Stand Podcast episode #027!

Day 12:

Daily Quote: "Broken Crayons Still Color" - Unknown

Personal Insight: The old Lauri would ALWAYS say, "I'm not creative". I have said this my entire life and believed that without a shadow of a doubt that it was true. I wasn't upset by it, it was simply who I was - or so I thought. What I learned after following Elizabeth Johnston with Own Your Creativity and doing the workbook called The Artist's Way by Julia Cameron is that I am SERIOUSLY CREATIVE!! My perception was just screwed up.

What I meant to say was that I hated scrapbooking, sewing, and doing "crafts". It just didn't do it for me. But because I didn't like those things when others did, siblings did, mom did, friends did, etc. I just didn't consider myself a creative being. What a bunch of nonsense!

My creativity includes writing things like this 30-Day Power of Positivity Challenge, my weekly blogs, and this book. It includes my mad skills at organizing - did I mention I was an Organizational Freakazoid who doesn't own even one junk drawer? Talk about OCD! I love making my house into a home and decorating it with love and fun things. I love creatively solving problems and I'm ridiculously resourceful when looking for solutions.

My creativity comes through in ways I had never imagined and I would bet that you are creative. In fact, I KNOW you are. If you don't think you are then you just haven't looked closely enough and found your creative truth. I want you to OWN YOUR CREATIVITY!

Daily Challenge: Click here: http://juliacameronlive.com/ and listen to Julia Cameron's 2-minute video on her beliefs about creativity and spirituality. You are creative. "There is no such thing as a non-creative person."

Write down one thing that shows you own your creativity

_____.

Daily Song Recommendation: "Wrong" by Kimberley Locke

This song breaks down any barriers of expectations that others have on you or limitations you have put on yourself. Love who you are right here, right now!

Daily Resource: Click here and purchase The Artist's Way by Julia Cameron: http://amzn.to/2qLFlRK It will change your life, but it is a commitment. I had no idea this book was a workbook until I dove in. Brace yourself for work, fun, insights, and creativity!

The Artist's Way is the seminal book on the subject of creativity. An international bestseller, millions of readers have found it to be an invaluable guide to living the artist's life. Still as vital today—or perhaps even more so—than it was when it was first published one decade ago, it is a powerfully provocative and inspiring work. In a new introduction to the book, Julia Cameron reflects upon the impact of The Artist's Way and describes the work she has done during the last decade and the new insights into the creative process that she has gained. Updated and expanded, this anniversary edition reframes The Artist's Way for a new century.

Extra Credit: Listen to how I Own My Creativity on my friend Elizabeth Johnston's Podcast here: http://apple.co/2rvEoAP

Day 13:

Daily Quote: "Change is simply another opportunity for more opportunities." - Sharlene Hawkes

Personal Insight: I'm Mormon. The LDS church is worldwide and therefore is structured geographically into what we call

Stakes and Wards. For example, I am part of the Camarillo California Stake which consists of 8 wards all of which are framed by a geographical map with boundaries.

Just over a year ago, due to new houses being built, people moving in or out, etc. our boundaries all changed. I was so excited and was looking forward to the new boundaries! New friends, big changes, new faces…I was definitely excited! But there were some who weren't…and believe it or not, over a year later, are still upset over it!

Life is full of changes. This is but one example of a change in my life that brought new opportunities. New friends, new opportunities to serve, and honestly…faith-building for me. So what's the difference? Why was I excited with anticipation and others are still poo-pooing the idea over a year later? It's all about perception.

Perception is an intuitive recognition or appreciation, insight, or discernment. Your thoughts! Now, I know that we can get stuck in our own heads with our thoughts and feelings, but it is OUR JOB to discern them. We create the perception of our environment. What is your current perception? Are you seeing things in the negative light or the positive light?

I hate to bring up Pollyanna, but yes, I'm going to go there. (And if you haven't seen it…watch it!) Pollyanna was taught to see something good in everything. You have the power in you to do exactly the same thing. Did you catch that? YOU HAVE THE POWER. You.

Remember, "change is simply another opportunity for more opportunities". If you see it in a negative light, the opportunities that come from it will more than likely be negative experiences because that is what you're seeking.

However, if you see it in a positive light, the opportunities that come from it will be more positive experiences.

Daily Challenge: Is there something you've been hanging on to in a negative light? Can you really try hard to be a Pollyanna today and find something positive about it? I believe in you and know you can do it!

Negative Thought or Situation:

Positive Thought or Solution:

Daily Song Recommendation: "Something More" by Sugarland

This song talks about negative situations and how she needs less hard time and more bliss...do what it suggests and break out of your negative mold and find this bliss for you!

Daily Resource: EXCLUSIVE OFFER JUST FOR LEMONADERS! Believe it or not, Sharlene has 89 copies left of her out-of-print book and is selling them exclusively through Lauri's Lemonade Stand and guess what? She is signing each copy!! Get your signed copy today by going to http://www.laurislemonadestand.com/ and clicking the paypal button - such a screaming deal! Once they're gone, they're gone as this book is not scheduled for any other printings - this is it!

Sharlene Hawkes, author of Kissing a Frog, "Finding Comfort Outside Your Comfort Zone" and Miss America 1985 suggests taking the word *change* and replacing it with the word *adventure*. It creates an element of fun to replace the fear that sometimes creeps in thinking of self-change. Grab your signed copy of Sharlene's book today and rock your next adventure with confidence!

Extra Credit: Listen to Sharlene Hawkes podcast interview on Lauri's Lemonade Stand, Episode #055!

Day 14:

Daily Quote: "What you seek is seeking you." - Rumi

Personal Insight: While I believe Rumi was right in his quote, I believe we have to work for it. We cannot sit idly by and wait for things to find us. The underlying part of Rumi's quote says, "What YOU seek..." What does that mean? Looking around with a pair of binoculars? I don't think so and I don't think that's what its intended meaning was or is.

If we look up the word seek it says that it means to try to find or discover by searching or questioning. That means action! Active seeking! If we are actively seeking, then what we are seeking for will also be seeking us. Confusing? Don't worry...clarification is found in today's challenge!

Daily Challenge: The Gold-Digger or Goal-Digger List

I learned about this concept from Rebekah "Bex" Borucki with BexLife who credits Erin Stutland with Shrink Session Workout for the idea. We are going to use a combination of these ideas to create your own Goal Digger List.

First, set a timer for 5 minutes and create a list of "I Wants". This can be anything from financial, to love, to career, to fitness, or just plain big things like a house or a Tesla Model X. Anything your heart desires goes on this list! Don't be shy! Here's five of them that ended up on my list the first time I did it:

I want to be a presenter at Time Out for Women.

I want to finish my Louis L'amour novel collection.

I want to finish writing my first book in 2018.

I want a Tesla Model X in red.

I want a Bianchi and name her Bella.

Got your list? Great! Now set it aside for Step 2.

Second, set a timer for 5 minutes and create a list of "I Have to Offers". What do you have to give to the world? This can be things people thank you for, things you bring into the world. It can be a sense of humor or charitable donations to your charity of choice. Here's a list of 5 things I used on my first list:

I offer my ability to make others feel comfortable and happy around me.

I offer donations to PCRM and to my church.

I offer my positivity podcast for women.

I offer my organizational skills with fun and creativity.

I offer my smile and laughter through poetry.

Now here's the fun part!

I'd like you to take 5 things from your list and put them together to create your own Gold Digger Mantras. Here are a couple of examples from my list:

I want to be a presenter at Time Out for Women. I offer my ability to make others feel comfortable and happy around me.

I want to finish writing my first book in 2018. I offer my organizational skills with fun and creativity.

After you have your list of 5 (or even 10!) Gold Digger

Mantras that are made specifically for you, I want you to write them down. Every day I want you to choose one and repeat it five times. I do mine shortly after I wake up and do my morning pages and prayer. I sit in my studio chair with my eyes closed and my hands on my upper legs and repeat one of my mantras 5 times each.

I will let you know that two of the things on my initial list already came true! I may not understand exactly how it works or the inner workings of manifesting, but I do know that it works! Try it!

Daily Song Recommendation: "It's a Good Day" by Hilary Weeks

Truly optimistic song. Today IS a Good Day no matter what!

Daily Resource: Want to learn more about manifesting and meditation with your Gold Digger List? Here is Rebekah "Bex" Borucki's YouTube video on the subject: http://bit.ly/2sk3zHv

Day 15:

Daily Quote: "There's no difference between a pessimist who says, 'Oh, it's hopeless, so don't bother doing anything,' and an optimist who says, 'Don't bother doing anything, it's going to turn out fine anyway.' Either way, nothing happens." -Yvon Chouinard, founder of Patagonia

Personal Insight: I am Reality Driven. I get so annoyed with the concept of the glass being half full or half empty. The theory is that if you see the glass as half empty that you are pessimistic. If you see the glass as half full, an optimist. When you are reality driven (in my humble opinion) it's the same! It doesn't matter...it is both half full *and* half empty. Whether it is negative or positive is beside the point - it is both and you are still stuck with half a glass of water!

The point here is that sometimes we need to change our view and find a working solution. The appropriate question should be, "What are you going to do with your glass?" or "What do you want from your glass?" All the amount of positive thinking will not fill the rest of that glass - action is needed. Maybe the water is tainted and you don't want it at all - throw it out! Both things require action.

Daily Challenge: Reality Check Ahead! Actions speak louder than words. We could sit around all day staring at the half full/half empty glass of water and have a philosophical conversation about optimism and pessimism, but the fact remains that it is still a glass of water that is both half full AND half empty.

Today's challenge is just to get you out of your own way. Get outside of your normal routine. Do something different. See things in a different light. If you never make your bed, make it. Or try this, don't! (That would be oh so much harder for me!) If you always order the same thing for lunch or dinner, try something new from the menu. Do you always watch TV when you get home in the evening? Try going for a walk instead or listening to music. Sit in a different chair at your dining room table. This is YOUR life, are you who you want to be?

Daily Song Recommendation: "This Is Your Life" by Switchfoot

Daily Resource: This amazing book: Operation Happiness by Kristi Ling! In Operation Happiness, happiness strategist and life coach Kristi Ling teaches you how to create immediate, positive shifts in your life by proving that *happiness is a skill that can be cultivated, learned, and mastered-much like playing an instrument.* Part memoir and part how-to, Operation Happiness combines compelling personal stories, inspiring perspective shifts, and big ah-ha moments with specific how-to's and clear actionable steps to help you create a solid foundation for sustainable happiness that will propel you into a new, light-filled way of living. Order yours here: http://www.operationhappinessbook.com/

Extra Credit: Listen to Kristi Ling's interview on Lauri's Lemonade Stand Podcast episode #006!

Day 16:

Daily Quote: "Everybody has a chapter they don't read out loud." - Unknown

Personal Insight: I was recently speaking at a church function and a woman came up to me afterwards and said, "I had no idea you were going through such tough things, you always just look like you have the perfect life." What? Welcome to social media, folks! I definitely do not air my dirty laundry in public if I happen to have any at the moment, but like the quote says "everybody has a chapter they don't read out loud". Including me. Including you. The point is that you don't need to share it out loud if that is uncomfortable to you, but the lesson is that you should be kind to everyone because you may never know about their unknown chapter. Embrace the whole person for what you do know, and for what you will never see. Everyone is going through something, period.

Daily Challenge: Embrace someone you might never have thought you would like. Have you judged someone lately? Don't beat yourself up over it, it's happened to the best of us. But do something kind for that person today. Open a door, love them for their differences.

Extra Tip and Food for Thought: Don't ever say something about someone else that you couldn't say if they were standing right in front of you. Just thinking about this statement will help you be more kind to those around you.

Daily Song Recommendation: "Freckles" by Natasha Bedingfield

I love this song because it celebrates freckles! I have always loved my freckles! Have you ever had your make-up done in in the mall? At the Nordstrom make-up counter for example? The first thing they want to do is cover up my freckles and hide my wrinkles. I earned those wrinkles, darling!

Another example, my youngest daughter (my mini-me) inherited my freckles. She is a Licensed Electrologist and one of her client's actually said to her, "I know a wonderful foundation that can hide those for you." She truly thought she was being helpful when I had taught my daughter to embrace her freckles. She loves them and wouldn't think of covering them up. It seemed like crazy talk to her - and it was.

Toss your self-doubt, embrace you. "A face without freckles is like a sky without the stars, why waste a second not loving who you are? Those little imperfections make you beautiful, lovable, valuable, they show your personality." Now, embrace others the same way.

Daily Resource: 21-Day Mantra Challenge by Rebekah "Bex" Borucki

In all fairness, you might want to wait until you're done with this 30-Day challenge before starting a new 21-Day challenge with Bex, but I just LOVED this 21-Day mantra challenge and Bex is wonderful! Check it out here: http://www.bexlife.com/21mantras/

Extra Credit: Listen to Rebekah Borucki's interview on Lauri's Lemonade Stand Podcast episode #043!

Day 17:

Daily Quote: "Life is thickly sown with thorns, and I know of no remedy other than to pass through them quickly. The longer we dwell on misfortunes, the greater is their power to harm us." - Voltaire

Personal Insights: This is a tough one for me to talk about and I'm sure that if you have a similar malady that you have spent way too much time dwelling on it, fretting over it, feeling guilty over it, or maybe even grieving over it. You can't choose your family.

This is tough because I tried for so many years to fix a couple of these broken relationships. I felt guilt and shame over them. We would get angry with each other over things and hold things over each other, ignore it for a certain amount of time, dip our toes in the water to see if it was ok to get back in and swim, only to have the same thing happen again and the cycle continued - for decades.

The blessing of a happy, well-adjusted marriage where I was able to learn more about myself and grow into the person that I love now allows me to choose to have relationships with people who love me as I am. Without judgment, without guilt, without never living up to unrealistic expectations and realizing that miserable people like to make others around them miserable.

Toxic relationships can be just that - toxic. If you look up toxic in the dictionary it talks of it being poison, causing unpleasant feelings that can be harmful or malicious.

Now don't get me wrong, I believe that families are and can be wonderful. I believe that families are the perfect environment to learn how to get along with others and find mutual respect and even admiration, but as adults we get to choose if we allow others to abuse these relationships.

We are designed to heal through healthy relationships, but the beauty of being an adult woman is that we can then choose those relationships. I upset the apple cart when I decided to break the cycle in my unhealthy relationships. It was seen as foreign and therefore wrong. But it was also freeing and let the weight of the world be lifted from my shoulders.

I did not come to this decision lightly nor do I hope that it is permanent - maybe someday we will find mutual ground! Lots and lots of thought and meditation and prayer (and therapy) went into this decision. But breaking the cycle has given me wings and I was the only one who had the power inside of me to do it.

You have the power inside of you to fix it or set it free.

Daily Challenge: Today's challenge is to try meditation. If you are already a user of this gift - I congratulate you! It isn't for everyone so don't feel like you need to jump on board once you try today's challenge. No pressure! (I still don't meditate myself, but I pray and do yoga so if that's what does it for you - great!)

Download the app HeadSpace. It has 10 free days of meditation and just do Day 1. Alternatively, you could look up the daily resource below as "Bex" shows you how even 4 minutes per day can change your life if you let it!

While you are meditating, contemplate a relationship that you need to either mend or let go. Is there something you could do today to get you on the path towards the relationships you want to cultivate or the one you need to let go for you to heal?

Daily Song Recommendation: "Power Inside of Me" by Richard Marx

Daily Resource: Bex's book - 4 Minutes to Change Your Life found here: http://www.bexlife.com/book/

In this book, Bex shows readers how to create a simple, practical, no-nonsense meditation practice that can fit into even the busiest schedules. Bex also shares powerful stories of how she healed her own anxiety and depression with meditation. Readers will come away with answers to commonly asked questions ("Do my eyes have to stay closed?" "What do I do if my body starts to hurt?"); technical information about props, postures, and mantras; and tools to cope with complex issues such as grief, body acceptance, and relationships.

Extra Credit: Listen to Rebekah "Bex" Borucki's interview on Lauri's Lemonade Stand Podcast episode #043!

Day 18:

Daily Quote: "If you wouldn't say it to your friend, don't say it to yourself." - Unknown

Personal Insight: There is an exercise that I do with my

audiences that talks about being your own best friend. I tell the audience that for the next few minutes they are collectively my "best friend". I let them know that I've had a poor body image, that I think of myself as fat, I hate my muffin-top, and that I pretty much feel ugly. I then ask them for their advice or simply what would they say to me if we were best friends and we were talking one-on-one.

It never fails. One of the first two things someone says is, "You're beautiful!" Oh, there's lots of great insights that come after that, but I always get "you're beautiful" in the top two. Think about that for a moment. If that's the first thing we would tell our best friends, why is it so hard to give ourselves that same advice?

We are consumed by negative self-talk. We plant that seed and then help it grow daily. But negativity is like a weed, and we are flowers. Different types and varieties, but flowers just the same. Don't treat yourself like a weed and help it grow. Yank that thing out of the ground and plant a flower seed instead.

Daily Challenge: May I suggest we treat that plant like a weed and yank it out! Don't spray weed killer or trim it down. This thing needs to be yanked by its roots so that it won't grow back.

Today we return to the mirror. Trust me, this gets easier. If you have had one little inkling of a thought of negativity about your body image today I want you to create an affirmation to its opposite. Here's an example:

If your negative self-talk was, "I'm so fat" your affirmation would be something like, "I am beautiful right here, right now. I am loved, worthy of love, and give love in abundance to others."

Try it! Use this one, or create your own, but then I want you to say this affirmation 5 times to yourself in the mirror. I believe that you are beautiful and that your thoughts are the key to changing negative self-talk into positive self-talk.

Daily Song Recommendation: "Think Good Thoughts" by Colbie Caillat

This song absolutely epitomizes the challenge for today - just enjoy!

Daily Resource: Meet my friend, Samantha Russell who is an eating psychology coach extraordinaire! She has an awesome freebie on her website called, "Fall in Love with Yourself - 15 Things You Can Do Today because yes, You Can Learn Self-Love" It's as easy as clicking right here: https://livethewhole.com/fall-in-love-with-yourself/

Extra Credit: Listen to Sam's interview on Lauri's Lemonade Stand Podcast episode #058!

Day 19:

Daily Quote: "You are allowed to be both a masterpiece and a work in progress, simultaneously." - Sophia Bush

Personal Insight: If we were to get together and sit at a round table, much like the knights of the round table did long ago and lay all of our troubles, past and present in the middle of the table, would you trade yours with someone else's? My bet is that we would all gather up our own troubles, both past and present, and not want to walk in anyone else's shoes.

We would be grateful for what our past troubles had taught us in becoming the person we are today - a masterpiece. We would pluck up our present troubles and realize that we are a work in progress, too. We are allowed to be both a masterpiece and a work in progress at the same time.

Daily Challenge: Write down 1 challenge you had in our past and journal about what you learned from it. Then pick one of your present troubles and find a silver lining. What are learning right now?

Daily Song Recommendation: "Born to Fly" by Hilary Weeks

This song is meant to make you feel like you were truly born to fly! You were meant to soar!

Daily Resource: Still not convinced that you wouldn't trade places with someone else? Still comparing your troubles to someone else's? Let me introduce you to my friend, Ashlee Birk who had what some people would call a perfect marriage, beautiful children, and was a stay-at-home mom until the police showed up at her door to tell her husband had been murdered. And while that would be enough and more to handle, learns that the reason he was shot and murdered was because he was having an affair she didn't know about with his married secretary whose husband decided that wasn't ok and came to murder Ashlee's husband that night.

Ashlee decided after lots of time and trauma that she needed to help other women through their trauma as well. Enter her website and conferences here: http://www.areasontostand.com/. I've had the privilege of attending and speaking at two of her conferences now and would highly recommend attending yourself. If you can't attend, please check out her books here: http://amzn.to/2qZWDeJ

Extra Credit: Listen to Ashlee Birk's interview on Lauri's Lemonade Stand Podcast episode #023!

Day 20:

Daily Quote: "If it doesn't open, it's not your door." - Unknown

Personal Insight: Do you ever have those days when everything you planned didn't go as planned? I know that one of my biggest pet peeves is when things don't go as planned. I'm late for a meeting, I didn't complete my daily reading, I had to postpone something until later in the day or simply to another day or my dreaded worst - it just doesn't happen.

And then something magical happens. Here's an example of the magic - I didn't do my daily reading the day before, but then I wake up the next day and the passage or chapter I read is exactly what I needed to hear that very moment. Another example - I was late for a meeting and missed a major traffic accident because I needed to take a different direction other than my usual route. And one more - the thing I needed to postpone ended up being a much better solution as more insights poured in.

I've learned to trust. Trust that I am exactly where I am supposed to be. That I am doing the best I can and that I am blessed and watched over in my journey. The minute you accept the fact that God or your creator or your higher power has your better good in mind, expect the universe to support your dream. It will.

Daily Challenge: Synchronicity to me are happy coincidences or happy connections. Look up synchronicity at dictionary.com and look at definition #5. Think about it for a moment. Now look for moments of synchronicity in your life

- past or present. Learn to pay attention. It really is fun and remarkable how many happy coincidences happen in our lives.

Daily Song Recommendation: "This Year" by Chantal Kreviazuk

I found this song, believe it or not, in the movie called Serendipity! Another word (and movie) that I LOVE! It speaks to positivity right here, right now!

Daily Resource: The book, *better each day* by Jessica Cassity http://amzn.to/2soeZr9

Its hundreds of tips add up to a big impact on well-being. Using the latest scientific findings from experts in the fields of nutrition, mental health, fitness, and psychology, respected journalist Jessica Cassity presents 365 proven and easy-to-achieve tips for feeling more confident, getting fit, clearing away worry and fear, improving relationships, and much more. Readers can work the tips day by day, or dip in and out of the book at will. With fascinating facts on the science behind self-improvement, this is an engaging and inspiring read perfect for anyone looking to feel healthier, and, of course, happier!

I use this book as a daily journal prompt. I read the short few paragraphs for the day and then write my thoughts and feelings on the subject. I give my opinion quite freely in my journals!

SOCIAL: RELATIONSHIPS

Are you ready? You've got this!! Now that you have focused on the psychological and physical aspects of your life over the last few weeks I hope that you are feeling ready to venture out and apply what you've learned into some of your relationships!

The last 10 days of this challenge are all about your relationships from strangers and neighbors, to spouses and family, and even if you're single and need a better relationship with yourself. Buckle up, cause it might be a bumpy ride! (I hope not, but relationships are where we learn to have better relationships - I hope that most of this is just smooth-sailing!)

Day 21: Strangers

Daily Quote: "Kindness is a language that the deaf can hear and the blind can see." - Mark Twain

Personal Insight: I am not Mother Teresa. That lady was a saint! But she knew how to treat complete and utter strangers with kindness. In her book, A Simple Path, she talks about this service. The Simple Path is this:

The fruit of silence is prayer,

The fruit of prayer is faith,

The fruit of faith is love,

The fruit of love is service,

The fruit of service is peace.

It is indeed a simple path. But simplicity does not always equal easy, does it? It is all well and good to spout off quotes and read books, but it is only in the action we take that differences in people's lives are made.

Daily Challenge: Today is a simple challenge that pushes you *slightly* out of your comfort zone and will not bring you any glory from the outside world. Only you will know the good you've done. Today you will perform two acts of kindness for complete strangers.

Now don't freak out! You've got this!

Challenge 1: It's time for Starbucks or Jamba Juice! Treat yourself to a sweet treat and put $5 towards the next person's bill. Tell the barista or the cashier to please hold your $5 until you leave and then once you're gone to apply it to the next person's bill. (This way, they are unable to thank you) This is your good deed that only you will know about. Ya know... like ding-dong ditching when you were a kid! I promise it will be the best $5 you spend all day!

Challenge 2: Perform a small act of service for a complete stranger. This can be as simple as holding a door for someone, picking up something that someone dropped, smiling at the next stranger you pass. No money involved with this one. I promise that if you seek out the opportunity, the opportunity will present itself.

Daily Song Recommendation: "Beautiful Life" by Mercy River

Daily Resource: Mother Teresa's Book, A Simple Path which you can buy here: http://amzn.to/2scV69q

Day 22: Friends

Daily Quote: "To have a friend, you must be a friend." - Lor-Lor

Personal Insight: You're gonna love this one! Have you ever felt like you weren't part of the group? Whether it was a social group, church group, work group, friend group? Well, I did! Remember on an earlier day when I talked about how our church was split up by geographical locations? Well, when I first moved to this beautiful town of Camarillo we were renting a house. We were there for 4 years and we loved our church family! We felt right at home, loved, cared for, no social clicks to worry about...you get the idea.

Then we bought a house. Now, buying a house is a good thing! Except that it moved us clear across town. My church family changed. Not the foundational principles, not how Sunday School was ran, but ALL OF THE FACES changed. And as hard as I tried, I just couldn't seem to fit in or make friends. It wasn't as if someone had offended me or done anything bad towards me, but I just didn't feel part of the group. I made one friend and asked her if she ever felt that way and she said she'd been living in that church boundary for years and still felt like I did! What? That's not right!

I'm not one to sit around and do nothing and if you know me even a little bit at this point, you know that I need to take action. So that's exactly what we did. We decided that if we wanted friends, that we needed to be a friend. And here's the fun part! We made a list of 10 questions to help us learn about someone new. Then when we arrived at church on Sunday we would sit in the back, whisper and point, and pick someone that we wanted to get to know better. Our plan was if we got to know them better that it would be easier to say hello and socialize more at church...and it worked!

We would set up a "date" with our next victim and then ask them those 10 questions to get to know them better. The next time we saw them we felt a connection and our "friend-ship" grew. We invited many others on to our "friend-ship" and it solved our problem. We knew that we were in charge of our own fate and that to have friends, we needed to be a good friend. If we sat around and just whined about it or had a pity-party then it would never be resolved. I've said it once, and I'll say it again, "to have a friend, you need to be a friend."

Daily Challenge: Is there someone you could invite onto your "friend-ship" today or even this week? If you need to use our example above, do it! Today I would like you to at least make a plan to be-friend someone. This doesn't mean you have to be bosom buddies or besties, in fact you can even invite one of your current friends with you to make the new connection if that makes you feel more comfortable, but you should at minimum make the plan today. Remember, that you never truly know what people are going through and you reaching out could be the best thing that happens to them all day!

Disclaimer: If it goes horribly wrong (I've never seen that happen), don't beat yourself up over it. Just like anything else in life, it just takes practice. Don't give up, be brave, and try it again!

Daily Song Recommendation: "Brave" by Sara Bareilles

No explanation needed for the song recommendation today - BE BRAVE!

Daily Resource: The Book, *There is No Good Card for This: What to Say and Do when Life is Scary, Awful, and Unfair to People you Love* by Kelsey Crowe. I cannot say enough good things about this book. Do you have a friend that has gone through something terrible or at least socially awkward? A divorce, loss, unemployment, coming out, break-up, parenthood, illness? Kelsey actually teaches empathy classes to help people learn how to react in these situations. If you first want to dip your toe in the water, she has amazing resources available RIGHT NOW on her website: http://www.helpeachotherout.com/

Extra Credit: Listen to Kelsey's interview on Lauri's Lemonade Stand Podcast episode #044!

Day 23: Be a Lantern - Being Assertive

Daily Quote: "Sometimes it takes an overwhelming breakdown to have an undeniable breakthrough."

Personal Insight: That was me...letting things build up and build up until I ultimately would just breakdown. I simply couldn't take on or handle one more thing in my particular relationship. And I'm not just talking about intimate relationships with a spouse, but even immediate family relationships that revolved around unresolved issues that stemmed from decades of discord.

In general, I'm a pretty easy-going individual. I get along and am comfortable around all sorts and types of people. And they are comfortable around me for the most part. I like to make people laugh and feel good about themselves (duh! Look at the health and happiness business I'm in! - it's what I live for!)

But sometimes things don't go as planned and you do not

have control of how others feel or act. If that were true, I would have had perfect children who did exactly what they were told all the time and I would have been a perfect child to my dear mother. Sorry mom…I know I put you through hell! (Seriously messed up teenager back in the day…)

However, all of my mistakes led me here and I LOVE who I am today! Oh, I'm not perfect, but I have learned so much about myself through all of my trials and really LOVE the lessons I've learned so far. My breakdowns have most definitely been breakthroughs for me.

Daily Challenge: Watch this 28-minute long video on Recognizing and Healing from Manipulative Relationships: Art of Connection by clicking here: http://www.drjuliehanks.com/category/relationship-advice-family/relationships/

Daily Song Recommendation: "Fight Song" by Rachel Platten

This song is my motivation when I need a little extra oomph in my day. It fires me up, has me singing out loud and in the end? Smiling and getting back on track from whatever had thrown me off.

Daily Resource: Love this book! *The Assertiveness Guide for Women: How to Communicate Your Needs, Set Healthy Boundaries, and Transform Your Relationships* by Dr. Julie Hanks. Order yours today by clicking here: http://amzn.to/2s8qQeX

Description: Isn't it time you took a stand? Many women struggle with assertiveness, but if you're prone to anxiety and avoidance, it is especially difficult. Grounded in attachment theory, this essential guide will help you identify your thoughts and feelings, balance your emotions, communicate your needs, and set healthy boundaries to improve your life.

Extra Credit: Listen to Dr. Julie Hank's interview on Lauri's Lemonade Stand Podcast episode #033!

Day 24: Marriage Relationships

Daily Quote: "Everyone comes with baggage. Find someone who loves you enough to help you unpack." - Unknown

Personal Insight: I like to say that when I married my husband that I came with "designer" baggage. And it was true! After feeling completely defeated after multiple failed marriages (yes, I went there), I still felt like I was a great catch. I AM a great catch! What has been interesting to me in finding someone who loves me for who I am, is that over ten years of looking back and insight makes me truly believe that my hubby indeed helped me to unpack. My marriage relationship has healed me because he has allowed me to grow into the best version of myself (so far!).

Daily Challenge: If you are currently in a loving relationship right now, the challenge is to do a little something for them today. Something that would speak to them, not you. Would your wife prefer a bouquet of wildflowers or a new drill for her project slumbering in the garage? Would your hubby appreciate a great massage or perhaps just sitting by him with a tub of popcorn and watch a movie of his choice? Do something kind for your significant other today. Even if you feel they don't deserve it.

Daily Song Recommendation: "Free" by Faith Hill

I love this song because it "Frees" you from whatever your past may have been and propels you into your future. A future where *you* are in control of your destiny. Your fate is in your own hands. It talks about unpacking your baggage and finding your own lovable self right there where it's been all along. Ready to put on your own pair of ruby slippers? (See song for reference)

Daily Resource: Many years ago we had an affluent couple invite us to a Valentine's Day dinner with lots of other couples and after serving a delectable meal announced that the entertainment for the evening would be a movie and we all moved upstairs to their theater room and settled in. What we didn't know was that they had an ulterior motive for the evening. The movie was called FireProof and it came with a lesson and a 40-Day Love Dare challenge. I don't want to ruin the story, but if your marriage relationship is in trouble or simply just needs a re-boot I recommend both the movie and the book PRONTO! Learn more by clicking here: http://amzn.to/2r7dsaH

Day 25: Work Relationships

Daily Quote: "You can't keep kicking a dead horse and then be surprised when it doesn't wake up." - Unknown

Personal Insight: I have held A LOT of jobs over my adult life. From Burger King Drive-Thru Queen at age 18 to a volunteer position when I was a Navy Wife called Ombudsman during the 9/11 crisis which is basically a liaison between the ship and the families back home. I've held numerous multi-level marketing jobs like Pampered Chef rep and even Amway for a very short stint! Got my real estate license and worked as a residential property manager for apartments all over Southern California and then managed a vehicle wrap shop in Riverside. Throw in a little stint at being a Stay-At-Home mom for 9 years and I've obviously run the gamut - and I loved MOST of it!

Here is what I learned: One, it's ok to switch jobs and that you grow from each one. Two, I learned how to be a good salesman in just being sincere and treating people well. The best tip I learned in the beginning? Smile when you're on the phone! The person on the other end can literally "feel" and "hear" your smile! Three, I learned how to troubleshoot work relationships and be direct. I'm not afraid to say what I need to say. Four, if I didn't like my job there was always something else better.

Do you love your job? Your workplace? Now, this note of encouragement is not to make you go out and quit today just because you don't love it. But perhaps it's an eye-opener to seeing your current job as your investor for a future job. OR, you might be able to simply fix the workplace you're in just by changing your attitude and putting on that smile!

Daily Challenge: Today I'd like you to go and visit my friend's website: https://reganwalsh.com/blog/ and read one of her blogs. Any one that jumps out at you will do. I especially like "Trust Your Gut" from 6/2/17, "Opportunity Knocks" from 5/15/17, and "How to Dream as an Adult" from 4/5/17 which features not only Regan Walsh, but Whitney Johnson both of whom have been on the podcast!

Daily Song Recommendation: "I Came to Win" by Jenny Jordan Frogley

Daily Resource: The Book: The Go-Giver by Bog Burg and John David Mann

I just can't give anything away with this book, because it is one that needs to be experienced, not just told about. Here are the words directly from the inside cover of the book:

The Go-Giver tells the story of an ambitious young man named Joe who yearns for success. Joe is a true go-getter, though sometimes he feels as if the harder and faster he works, the further away his goals seem to be. And so one day, desperate to land a key sale at the end of a bad quarter, he seeks advice from the enigmatic Pindar, a legendary consultant referred to by his many devotees simply as the Chairman.

Over the next week, Pindar introduces Joe to a series of "go-givers": a restaurateur, a CEO, a financial adviser, a real estate broker, and the "Connector", who brought them all together. Pindar's friends share with Joe the Five Laws of Stratospheric Success and teach him how to open himself up to the power of giving.

Joe learns that changing his focus from getting to giving - putting others' interests first and continually adding value to their lives - ultimately leads to unexpected returns.

Imparted with wit and grace, The Go-Giver is a heartwarming and inspiring tale that brings new relevance to the old proverb "Give and you shall receive."

Extra Credit: Listen to Regan's interview on Lauri's Lemonade Stand Podcast episode #040 or Whitney's episode #25!

Day 26: Being Single Part 1

Daily Quote: "Start where you are." - Dieter F Uchtdorf

Personal Insight: I sucked at single. I admit it. I let my parents divorce when I was 11 years old dictate how I would show up in relationships (horribly and without a clue) for the next 2+ decades of my life so I am not one to give advice on being single at all.

However, I want to be sensitive to the fact and not ignore that some of us are single as heck! Now whether you've chosen that position yourself or felt like it's a life-long sentence, it doesn't change the fact you're single and I want to give you an incredible resource (if not somewhat vulgar and direct) to navigate your way.

Daily Challenge: Whether you are single by choice and want to stay that way, or you are desperate to be in a relationship, Kira Sabin with The League of Adventurous Singles is bomb at coaching singles. Today's challenge is simple: Check out Kira's blog here: http://leagueofadventuroussingles.com/blog/. Choose a blog that speaks to you and read it! Leave her a comment while you're at it and let her know what you thought!

Disclaimer: Kira uses straight up vulgar language on her website. If that's not your thing, then be patient my dear Lemonader…I have one more singles resource for you tomorrow.

Daily Song Recommendation: "Keep'n It Real" by Shaggy

Daily Resource: Kira Sabin, League of Adventurous Singles FREE STUFF here: http://leagueofadventuroussingles.com/blog/free/ Kira has 2 amazing freebies on her website - descriptions here:

1) WHAT TO SAY WHEN YOU DON'T KNOW WTF TO SAY, Scripts for awkward dating situations.

Let's be honest…dating can get awkward. You may be

confident in the rest of your life, but when you throw in emotions, expectations and the like, we can get real nervous.

2) GETTING OVER YOUR PAST RELATIONSHIP WORKBOOK

YOU ARE IN A VERY IMPORTANT TIME OF YOUR LIFE. A time where you have important choices. One where you can glom onto the next mostly available person because you don't want to be alone, OR you can step back, learn from your past relationship, work on yourself and go in smarter, more confident and get what you need this time around. Doesn't that sound swell? I know it does.

Extra Credit: Listen to Kira's interview on Lauri's Lemonade Stand Podcast episode #051! (It's a clean version!)

Day 27: Being Single Part 2

Daily Quote: "Be Weird. Be Random. Because you never know who would love the person you hide." - C.S. Lewis

Personal Insight: Confession time: I don't like to travel. I am a homebody, love the comfort of my home, curl up on the couch or recliner with a good book or movie with my favorite french fries kinda gal. I travel for work as far as attending conferences and speaking engagements and have lived in 7 different states in the US including Hawaii for 3 years, but I don't have the travel bug.

My sister has it, several of my brothers have it, and my youngest daughter has it. Even my mom has it! But I stay pretty close to home. Then I interviewed Jennifer Buccholz from Transform via Travel and thought, "This sounds fun! I could do this!" Do you like to travel?

Daily Challenge: Jennifer with Transform via Travel teaches self-care through solo travel. If you have a desire to travel and be inspired, not to mention learn some more about yourself, please visit Jennifer's website here: https://www.transformviatravel.com/, go to the bottom and sign up for her FREE #YOLOGOSOLO 7-day inspiration + thought-provoking activity to release your fears and just go (solo).

Daily Song Recommendation: "Don't Hold Me Down" by Colbie Callait

Daily Resource: Transform via Travel by Jennifer Buccholz has a book that you are going to adore! *Go Solo!: A Savvy Woman's Guide to Transformation & Self - Discovery Through Trave*l By Jennifer I. Buchholz, Amy Oaks (Buy here; http://amzn.to/2soEJ9u) Here's the low-down:

Travel enthusiast and Life Coach Jennifer Buchholz will be your guide on your own personal journey of self-discovery in GO SOLO! Explore your personal why, when and where to go, and then how to actually make it happen! Jennifer shares personal experiences and insights from her own solo travels, as well as a series of activities to coax you gently out of your comfort zone, and toward who you are truly meant to be. You can travel solo with confidence-and experience new-found freedom and growth along the way. This book has a companion Travel Journal.

Day 28: Saying No in Your Relationships

Daily Quote: "No is a complete sentence."

Personal Insight: Oh boy, did it take me forever to learn this one! Maybe you are one of those people that have this natural born gift of saying no when you don't want to do something and saying yes when it feels good or right, but the rest of us have found it to be a learned art. It's something we've had to practice over and over again.

Sometimes the person we have to say no to is ourselves! We self-sabotage by taking on more and more in some insane attempt to prove to ourselves that we can take on more. Like it's a rite of passage or that we'll be seen as a superhero with superhero powers of being able to do everything all at once without batting a single eyelash. Why? Why do we do that?

Sometimes it's not being able to say no when people ask us to do something that we truly don't want to do and we resent it from the moment that "yes" falls out of our face when we really just wanted to scream no from the rooftops!

The truth of the matter is that we all want to be of service and help others in any way we can, but when you say yes often enough, people don't ask anyone but you because THEY KNOW YOU'LL SAY YES! Because you've never said no before!

Daily Challenge: Say no to something you really don't want to do. Even go as far as practicing in your mirror - "I'm not able to commit to that right now". "No, I can't do that. But here's what I can do…" " I'm going to say no for now…I'll let you know if anything changes."

(Credit to Dr. Julie Hanks with *The Assertiveness Guide for Women* for these!)

Daily Song Recommendation: "Lessons Learned" by Carrie Underwood

Daily Resource: Kristina Kuzmic's YouTube Video on Saying No: http://bit.ly/2senp71

Extra Credit: Listen to Kristina's interview on Lauri's Lemonade Stand Podcast episode #034!

Day 29: Relationship with Self - Of worth now.

Daily Quote: "worthy now. not if. not when. we are worthy of love and belonging now. right this minute. as is." - Brene Brown

Personal Insight: This is one of my favorite stories to tell when learning self-acceptance. I am a crier. I cry over everything. Happy moments, sad moments, angry moments, stressful moments, you get the idea. When I was married for just over a year with my truly amazing hubby, I had a moment...and I was crying. I was so frustrated by the hot tears rolling down my face that I had zero control over. I remember being so disgusted with myself and telling my sweet husband, "I'm going to learn to control this! I will get better at not crying!"

And then this happened: My husband looked contemplative and thoughtful for a moment and said the most amazing thing ever. "Honey, I've known you for a long time now and I don't think this part of you is going to change." What? It was ok to cry? To blubber even?

From that moment on, I have learned to embrace the fact that I cry at all sorts of things and that it's ok. I embrace it as a part of myself that isn't going to change. It is part of who I am and how I show up on this planet. I've embraced it and moved on. It was such a huge weight off of my shoulders that I had been beating myself up over for years and finally let it go.

In fact, I help coach a mountain bike team that is made up of middle school and high school student athletes and one of my middle school girls recently crashed hard and was trying desperately to hold back the tears. I let her know that crying is absolutely ok and even would help release the pressure of emotions that had built up in those few moments of crashing, feeling embarrassed and just plain physically hurting from the bumps and bruises.

She let it out, cried it out, and guess what? Felt better!

Daily Challenge: Is there something that is obviously a part of you that you feel is a burden or a shameful thing that you can just let go and embrace in yourself today? Maybe it's the fact that you have freckles (I have them and love them! I bet yours are amazing, too!) or that you feel guilty for owning too many pairs of shoes (someone just brought that up last week - no joke) or someone is bugging you about getting rid of some of your books because THEY THINK you have too many, but you love them (keep them for heaven's sake!).

Whatever it is, pick something that you know other people might bug you for or that you've beat yourself up over for far too long and let that sh** go. You do you...you're the only one that can.

Daily Song Recommendation: "Just Like Fire" by Pink

No one can do you like you - this song embraces that with all the fire that Pink can muster!

Daily Resource: This book: *The Gifts of Imperfection: Let Go of Who You Think You're Supposed to Be and Embrace Who You Are* by Brene' Brown. No description needed, just click here and buy now: http://amzn.to/2rMeSqT

Day 30: Embrace Yourself - Show Up Boldly in the World with Confidence Now!

Daily Quote: "Procrastination is the grave in which opportunity is buried." - Unknown

Personal Insight: Congratulations! I can't believe we are already on the last day of this 30-Day Power of Positivity Challenge! Crazy!

Remember that feeling on the last day of school and everyone is practically jumping out of their own skin in anticipation of summer vacation? I want you to find that feeling from your youth and celebrate it! It's time for #Recess!!

Recess is an important part of our everyday life. Little daily breaks and then weekly #PlayDates need to be a part of our make-up. Let's embrace recess again!

Daily Challenge: Plan a date just for yourself! First, set the date and time and give yourself at least 2 hours - more is better! What are you going to do? Go roller-skating in old school roller skates at the local Skate Rink? Go to that movie that came out last week and you're dying to go see? Eat at your favorite restaurant or just order it take-out and binge watch a season of Gilmore Girls or Arrow? Set the date and time right now and don't let procrastination get in your way. Say no to other things if you need to. Protect this time with yourself - you deserve recess.

Daily Song Recommendation: "Don't Give Up" by Eagle-Eye Cherry

Don't give up - never give up. (This song was not available on iTunes, so please look it up on Vimeo and watch instead.)

Daily Resource: Need ideas on self-dates? Check out this link to my blog that gives you 5 tried and true, tested by me dates that will give you some more ideas! - http://bit.ly/2tmkRAw

Now that you're a seasoned veteran of the 30-Day Power of Positivity Challenge, come on over through social media and share your experience! I would love to hear from you and thank you from the bottom of my heart for trying out this method of healing and happiness. Wishing you love and blessings wherever this finds you, my fellow Lemonader and friend.

Stay in Touch!

Website/Subscriber List: laurislemonadestand.com

Facebook: @laurislemonadestand

Instagram: @kugsnhisses

Twitter: @laurimackey

DISCLOSURE: Many of the product links in this challenge are affiliate links for companies and individuals that I have business relationships with. Clicking on these links and making a purchase sometimes results in a small payday for me. There are also many products mentioned with which I have no financial affiliation. Every product, program, and expert I recommend in this challenge has been personally vetted by me. You can rest assured that what you see is what you get.

To receive a pdf download version of the 30-Day Power of Positivity Challenge, please go to laurislemonadestand.com/challenge and get your very own, dolled up version of this challenge.

POSITIVITY PLAYLIST

"Best Day of My Life" by American Authors
"Change In The Making" by Mercy River
"Win The Day" by Hilary Weeks
"Love Your Life" by Hilary Weeks
"Brave" by Hilary Weeks
"Soul Stroll" by Erin Stutland
"Feel the Love" by Cahill & Kimberley Locke
"Born This Way" by Lady Gaga
"Shatter Me" by Lindsey Stirling
"I'm Coming Out" by Diana Ross
"Rock Bottom" by Wynonna Judd
"Wrong" by Kimberley Locke
"Something More" by Sugarland
"It's A Good Day" by Hilary Weeks
"This Is Your Life" by Switchfoot
"Freckles" by Natasha Bedingfield
"Power Inside of Me" by Richard Marx
"Think Good Thoughts" by Colbie Caillat
"Born To Fly" by Hilary Weeks
"This Year" by Chantal Kreviazuk
"Beautiful Life" by Mercy River
"Brave" by Sara Bareilles
"Fight Song" by Rachel Platten
"Free" by Faith Hill
"I Came to Win" by Jenny Jordan Frogley
"Keep'n It Real" by Shaggy
"Don't Hold Me Down" by Colbie Callait
"Lessons Learned" by Carrie Underwood
"Just Like Fire" by Pink
"Don't Give Up" by Eagle-Eye Cherry

ABOUT LAURI MACKEY

Lauri Mackey, Certified Holistic Health Coach and positivity crusader is the proprietor of Lauri's Lemonade Stand, a Positivity Podcast for Women. Lauri studies and teaches The Art of Holiatry which focuses on 3 main points of health and well-being: Physical which includes nourishment and movement, Psychological which includes your mind and spirit, and then how to bring that best self into the third branch of Social which is how you show up in your relationships. Lauri's unique background of struggle through experience has her shouting from the rooftops that if she can make it, anyone can!

It took Lauri a long time to figure out how to show up as her best self, most of which happened after age 40 as a matter of fact. All after age 40, Lauri has graduated high school, earned a certificate in Plant-Based Nutrition through eCornell University, became a Certified Holistic Health Coach through IIN, established Lauri's Lemonade Stand including a successful interview-based podcast, became a public speaker with training from YSU, and became a mountain bike coach for the local high school team. She's even raced her mountain bike and made it onto podiums! Lauri believes that it is never too late to start the next chapter of your life.

Lauri lives in Camarillo, CA where she podcasts from the studio in her home and lives with her best friend and husband, Eddy and their two dogs, Lakota and Kozmo. She is a mother of three grown daughters and a Gram to two beautiful grandchildren.

Follow Lauri on social media @laurislemonadestand on Facebook, @laurimackey on Twitter and her newest venture into Instagram @kugsnhisses. Sign up for her weekly emails on her website at laurislemonadestand.com and always check the events page to see if you can see her live and in person at her next speaking gig!

ACKNOWLEDGEMENTS

Thanks first to my experiences in life that brought me to writing this book.

Thanks also to my dear husband, Eddy, who allows me space to learn who I am and who I want to be when I grow up which to this day is still ever-changing. Not only is his love an anchor in my life, but his belief and support in me continues to carry me through whatever I've set my mind to next. Thank you for always helping me into the next chapter of my life.

Thanks to Heidi Resnik for taking the time for brutal editing. You are amazing at it!

Made in the USA
San Bernardino, CA
29 May 2018